MW00852475

SHAKESPEARE'S

MACBETH

WITH ANNOTATIONS, COMMENTARY,
AND ILLUSTRATIONS

MADELYN ROSE CRAIG

ROSEWOOD
PUBLISHING

ISBN: 978-1-7355711-5-7 (Hardcover)

ISBN: 978-1-7355711-6-4 (Paperback)

Rosewood Publishing
www.madelynrosecraig.com

Table of Contents

Editor's Note

All of my art teachers knew a particular quirk of my creations: I loved to draw birds. Granted, I was not always that great at capturing them, but I loved them. I even had a few pet birds over the years. I studied the birds outside my window, learned how to mimic their calls, and even kept a journal of all the birds I saw. Then in college, I was given the opportunity to find something unique in a work of Shakespeare. Believe it or not, birds were not the first theme to come to mind. Yet it was not long before they made their presence known. I have since expanded on that first collection, and I found more instances of flight and birds with each reading of this wonderful work. Yet there is even more to discover in *Macbeth*! While I love the bird imagery, I also love the other themes of marriage, family, fathers, and duty, and I note those themes as they arise. My comments and annotations in this edition are likely to be unusual. I wanted to give a snapshot of my mind as I read the play, what connections I made to other pieces of literature and Scripture, how a particular event impacted the rest of the play, historical or etymological contexts, and the deeper truths behind the various symbols, most especially in the birds and their winged friends — all points that add significant depth to the play. Most of all, I wanted to create an edition of *Macbeth* in a way that was accessible to new readers and intriguing to long-time readers of Shakespeare. With that in mind, read, learn, and enjoy this edited, modern First Folio edition of Shakespeare's *Macbeth*.

Glossary

Act

The major division in the play, typically split up by scenes.

Aside

An actor's lines spoken for the audience's benefit and unheard by the other actors on the stage, usually to demonstrate inner thought, unless as an aside to a specific character.

Blank Verse

A line in iambic pentameter that does not rhyme.

Comic Relief

A scene that allows the audience to have a break from a tragic moment with a light-hearted scene.

Couplet

A pair of lines in verse that rhyme, have the same meter, and conveys meaning within itself. Utilized by many poets, Shakespeare frequently included them in his plays.

Dramatic Irony

Also called tragic irony, originating in Greek dramas. To speak something that the audience understands or has additional information about but is not fully understood by or is unknown to the speaker.

Exeunt

Latin for *they go out*. Used in plays to indicate to the actors when they are to leave the stage.

Foil

A character used to contrast another character by having certain parallels in either nature or situation but acting in contrasting ways.

Foreshadowing

When an element is introduced in literature early on to indicate something that will happen later in the work, though the significance often isn't recognized until later.

Hamartia
   The tragic or fatal flaw of the hero that results in their downfall.

Heroic Couplet
   A couplet written in iambic pentameter often used in long forms of poetry or plays and typically found as a concluding and self-contained statement. Both lines are usually complete statements and can stand alone, but together convey a deeper meaning.

Iambic Pentameter
   A line of verse having five "feet' or iams for a total of ten syllables. This meter is most common in English poetry, including Shakespeare's plays and sonnets.

Scene
   A segment of a play, typically divided by time, location, or introduction of new characters or plot. They are often the subdivision of acts in a play.

Soliloquy
   The speech of a character when they are speaking to themselves when they are alone or when they think they are alone.

Tragedy
   A literary composition that deals with somber themes and characters, resulting in a change in fortune and often ending in fatal events.

Tragic hero
   A great character who falls or fails because of a fatal flaw, or hamartia.

The Tragedy of Macbeth

Dramatis Personæ

DUNCAN, King of Scotland
MALCOLM, his son
DONALBAIN, his son

MACBETH, Thane of Glamis, Cawdor, and later King of Scotland
LADY MACBETH

BANQUO, a thane
FLEANCE, his son

MACDUFF, Thane of Fife
LADY MACDUFF
SON

LENNOX, a thane
ROSS, a thane
MENTEITH, a thane
ANGUS, a thane
CAITHNESS, a thane

SIWARD, Earl of Northumberland
YOUNG SIWARD, his son

SEYTON, an officer attending Macbeth
ENGLISH DOCTOR
SCOTTISH DOCTOR
GENTLEWOMAN, for Lady Macbeth
CAPTAIN, for Duncan
PORTER
OLD MAN
MURDERERS
APPARITIONS
Other attendants, messengers, servants, lords, etc.
Three WITCHES or WEIRD SISTERS
HECATE

ACT I
SCENE I. An open place
Thunder and Lightning. Enter three Witches.

FIRST WITCH.
5   When shall we three[1] meet again?
     In thunder, lightning, or in rain?

SECOND WITCH.
     When the hurlyburly's[2] done,
     When the battle's lost and won.[3]

THIRD WITCH.
     That will be ere the set of sun.

FIRST WITCH.
     Where the place?

SECOND WITCH.
10   Upon the heath.[4]

THIRD WITCH.
     There to meet with Macbeth.

FIRST WITCH.
     I come, Grimalkin![5]

SECOND WITCH.
     Paddock[6] calls.

---

[1] The three Weird Sisters. Literally, the three fates. These three are in various mythologies, but Shakespeare probably derived his from the Anglo-Saxon mythology. Because these three were typically depicted as strange, frightening, or unearthly, the word "weird" came to mean odd, disturbing, or different.

[2] A tumult.

[3] Which battle lost? Which won? This is foreshadowing.

[4] An open, uncultivated area.

[5] Witch's familiar; a gray cat; a demon.

[6] A toad and witch's familiar.

THIRD WITCH.
    Anon.[7]

ALL.
15   Fair is foul, and foul is fair:[8]
    Hover through the fog and filthy air.

[Exeunt.][9]

---

[7] At once.

[8] This is reminiscent of Isaiah 5:20. Also, through half-truths they cloud the view of those they speak to.

[9] Short for "exeunt omnes," a Renaissance Latin phrase for "they all go out."

SCENE II. A camp near Forres

*Alarum[1] within. Enter King Duncan, Malcolm, Donalbain,[2] Lennox, with
attendants, meeting a bleeding Captain.*

DUNCAN.[3]

What bloody[4] man is that? He can report,
As seemeth by his plight, of the revolt
The newest state.

MALCOLM.[5]

This is the sergeant
Who like a good and hardy soldier fought
5   'Gainst my captivity.—Hail, brave friend!
Say to the King the knowledge of the broil
As thou didst leave it.

CAPTAIN.

Doubtful it stood,
As two spent swimmers that do cling together
And choke their art. The merciless Macdonwald[6]—
10   Worthy to be a rebel, for to that

---

[1] A trumpet call.

[2] I will include the meanings and etymologies of character's names from
time to time as names and their meanings are important to people, history,
and even fiction. While Donalbain gets no lines in this scene, it is the first
time he is mentioned. Donalbain: Dòmhnall bán: Dòmhnall/Donald the
fair (fair haired, perhaps). Dòmhnall: ruler of the world.

[3] Duncan: Donnchadh: Donn: brown; cath: battle.

[4] A curse and observation.

[5] Malcolm: Máel Coluim: disciple of St. Columba: dove. Besides the fact
that his name derives from the word dove, which is fascinating in the sense
that there is an abundance of birds in this play, St. Columba and the tradi-
tions surrounding his life also play a part in *Macbeth*. Born in Ireland in
521 A.D., he eventually became a monk and was later ordained. He
founded several monasteries, including the Abbey of Kells. After a terrible
event where the king of Ireland executed those claiming sanctuary with
Columba, he went on pilgrimage to Scotland. One of his miracles is that
he banished the monster of Loch Ness to its depths after attacking a man.
He lived on Iona, where he founded a monastery and school. He died in
597 A.D.

[6] The Thane of Cawdor. Once one of Duncan's trusted men but traitor-
ously allies with Norway.

The multiplying villainies of nature
Do swarm upon him—from the Western Isles[7]
Of kerns[8] and gallowglasses[9] is supplied;
And Fortune,[10] on his damnéd quarrel smiling,
15   Show'd like a rebel's whore. But all's too weak;
For brave Macbeth[11]—well he deserves that name—
Disdaining Fortune, with his brandished steel,
Which smok'd with bloody execution,
Like valour's[12] minion, carv'd out his passage,
20   Till he faced the slave,
Which ne'er shook hands nor bade farewell to him[13]
Till he unseam'd[14] him from the nave[15] to th'chops,[16]
And fix'd his head upon our battlements.

DUNCAN.
Oh, valiant cousin, worthy gentleman!

CAPTAIN.
25   As whence the sun 'gins his reflection[17]
Shipwrecking storms and direful thunders break,
So from that spring, whence comfort seem'd to come
Discomfort swells. Mark, King of Scotland, mark:
No sooner justice had, with valour arm'd,
30   Compell'd these skipping kerns to trust their heels,[18]
But the Norweyan[19] lord, surveying vantage,
With furbish'd arms and new supplies of men,

---

[7] The Hebrides, an archipelago off the west coast of Scotland; possibly also Ireland.

[8] Irish soldiers.

[9] Elite mercenary warriors.

[10] The goddesses, though here described as unfaithful.

[11] Macbeth: Mac Beatha: Son of life.

[12] Deified courage.

[13] Offered no pleasantries.

[14] An apt depiction of the brutality of war.

[15] The naval.

[16] The jaw.

[17] Begins to rise.

[18] To flee.

[19] Norwegian.

Began a fresh assault.

DUNCAN.
   Dismay'd not this
   Our captains, Macbeth and Banquo?[20]

CAPTAIN.
35   Yes, as sparrows eagles,[21] or the hare the lion.
   If I say sooth,[22] I must report they were
   As cannons overcharg'd with double cracks,
   So they doubly redoubled strokes upon the foe.
   Except they meant to bathe in reeking wounds,
40   Or memorize another Golgotha,[23]
   I cannot tell—
   But I am faint, my gashes cry for help.

DUNCAN.
   So well thy words become thee as thy wounds:
   They smack of honour both.—Go, get him surgeons.

                    [Exit Captain, attended.]

                    [Enter Ross and Angus.]

45   Who comes here?

---

[20] Banquo and Macbeth are both thanes of Scotland. Thanes are chiefs or lords in Scotland, whose property and jurisdiction is a thanedom or thanage. Banquo's thanage is never mentioned, but it appears he is based on the Thane of Lochaber from the *Holinshed's Chronicles*, from which Shakespeare draws this story. His historicity is highly questioned. Shakespeare also changed the role Banquo played in the murder of Duncan, perhaps to make a better foil or because of the patronage of King James VI & I (Consider 4.1). His name's meaning is unclear. Perhaps it comes from Ban: white/fair. Cu: hound. This would be interesting, considering what Macduff will eventually call Macbeth in 5.8. Also, Lochaber is in the tradition of St. Columba as the saint cared from a man from there.
[21] The first two birds of the play. Here, the rebels are described as weak sparrows where Macbeth and Banquo are fierce eagles.
[22] Tell the truth, fact. From Old English.
[23] Where Christ was crucified. Make the place as infamous as that spot of death. He is describing the ferocity of their fighting.

MALCOLM.
The worthy Thane of Ross.

LENNOX.
What a haste looks through his eyes!
So should he look that seems to speak things strange.

ROSS.
God save the King!

DUNCAN.
50   Whence cam'st thou, worthy thane?

ROSS.
From Fife, great King, where the Norweyan banners
Flout the sky and fan our people cold.
Norway himself, with terrible numbers,
Assisted by that most disloyal traitor,
55   The Thane of Cawdor,[24] began a dismal conflict;
Till that Bellona's[25] bridegroom, lapp'd in proof,[26]
Confronted him with self-comparisons,[27]
Point against point, rebellious arm 'gainst arm,
Curbing his lavish spirit. And, to conclude,
60   The victory fell on us.

DUNCAN.
Great happiness!

ROSS.
That now
Sweno, the Norways' king, craves composition;[28]
Nor would we deign him burial of his men

---

[24] Macdonwald.
[25] Roman goddess of war. Bellum: war.
[26] Macbeth in war-tested armor.
[27] They were a good match in skill.
[28] Desires to make a treaty.

Till he disburséd at Saint Colme's Inch[29]

65   Ten thousand dollars[30] to our general use.

DUNCAN.
No more that Thane of Cawdor shall deceive
Our bosom interest.[31] Go, pronounce his present death,
And with his former title greet Macbeth.[32]

ROSS.
I'll see it done.

DUNCAN.
70   What he hath lost, noble Macbeth hath won.

[Exeunt.]

---

[29] Inchcolm, the Isle of St. Columba on the east side of Scotland, where an abbey was later dedicated to him.
[30] Spanish or Dutch coins.
[31] There is irony in reading this with hindsight. Also, it is possible the audience experiencing this play in Shakespeare's day would have known the history, even in this fictionalized form.
[32] Macbeth is now also the Thane of Cawdor.

SCENE III. A heath near Forres

Thunder. Enter the three Witches.

FIRST WITCH.
Where hast thou been, sister?

SECOND WITCH.
Killing swine.

THIRD WITCH.
Sister, where thou?

FIRST WITCH.
A sailor's wife had chestnuts in her lap,
5   And munched, and munched, and munched. "Give me," quoth I.
"Aroint thee,[1] witch!" the rump-fed runnion[2] cries.
Her husband's to Aleppo gone, master o'th' *Tiger*;
But in a sieve I'll thither sail,
And, like a rat without a tail,
10   I'll do, I'll do, and I'll do.[3]

SECOND WITCH.
I'll give thee a wind.

FIRST WITCH.
Th'art kind.

THIRD WITCH.
And I another.

FIRST WITCH.
I myself have all the other,
15   And the very ports they blow,
All the quarters that they know
I'th'shipman's card.[4]
I'll drain him dry as hay.

---

[1] Begone.
[2] Trash eater.
[3] A sexual implication. These deformed beings bring evil and seduce.
[4] She will use all the winds from each quarter of the compass to sail.

11

Sleep shall neither night nor day
20 Hang upon his pent-house lid;[5]
He shall live a man forbid.[6]
Weary sev'nnights[7] nine times nine,
Shall he dwindle, peak,[8] and pine.
Though his bark cannot be lost,[9]
25 Yet it shall be tempest-tossed.[10]
Look what I have.

SECOND WITCH.
Show me, show me.

FIRST WITCH.
Here I have a pilot's thumb,
Wrack'd as homeward he did come.

[Drum within.]

THIRD WITCH.
30 A drum, a drum!
Macbeth doth come.

[Dancing in a circle.]

ALL.
The Weird Sisters, hand in hand,
Posters[11] of the sea and land,
Thus do go about, about,
35 Thrice to thine, and thrice to mine,
And thrice again, to make up nine.
Peace! The charm's wound up.[12]

---

[5] His eyelids.
[6] Accursed.
[7] Weeks.
[8] Become peaked, thin.
[9] They can't destroy his ship (bark), but they can send storms.
[10] Notice the rhyming in this section. They are chanting spells.
[11] Swift travelers.
[12] Ready.

MACBETH.
> So foul and fair[13] a day I have not seen.

BANQUO.
> How far is't call'd to Forres?—What are these,
40 So wither'd, and so wild in their attire,
> That look not like the inhabitants o'th'earth,[14]
> And yet are on't?—Live you? Or are you aught
> That man may question? You seem to understand me,
> By each at once her choppy[15] finger laying
45 Upon her skinny lips. You should be women,
> And yet your beards[16] forbid me to interpret
> That you are so.

MACBETH.
> Speak, if you can. What are you?

FIRST WITCH.
> All hail, Macbeth! Hail to thee, Thane of Glamis!

SECOND WITCH.
> All hail, Macbeth! Hail to thee, Thane of Cawdor!

THIRD WITCH.
50 All hail, Macbeth! That shalt be king hereafter![17]

BANQUO.
> Good sir, why do you start and seem to fear
> Things that do sound so fair?—I'th'name of truth,
> Are ye fantastical,[18] or that indeed

---

[13] Echoing the Sisters' phrase. Gruesome and successful.

[14] Describing the Sisters.

[15] Cracked.

[16] A literal beard, but otherwise appearing feminine in form. They show male and female elements, but they are neither man nor woman. This is demonic.

[17] Foreshadowing or warning of what is to come. One might say this becomes a self-fulfilling prophesy by suggestion.

[18] Illusions, fantasy, imaginations.

Which outwardly ye show? My noble partner
55 You greet with present grace[19] and great prediction
Of noble having and of royal hope,
That he seems rapt withal.[20] To me you speak not.
If you can look into the seeds of time,
And say which grain will grow and which will not,
60 Speak then to me, who neither beg nor fear
Your favours nor your hate.

FIRST WITCH.
Hail!

SECOND WITCH.
Hail!

THIRD WITCH.
Hail!

FIRST WITCH.
65 Lesser than Macbeth, and greater.[21]

SECOND WITCH.
Not so happy, yet much happier.[22]

THIRD WITCH.
Thou shalt get kings, though thou be none.[23]
So all hail, Macbeth and Banquo!

FIRST WITCH.
Banquo and Macbeth, all hail!

MACBETH.
70 Stay, you imperfect speakers,[24] tell me more.
By Sinel's[25] death I know I am Thane of Glamis;

---

[19] Current honor.
[20] Entranced.
[21] He is of lower status but higher character.
[22] Not as fortunate, but content and untroubled.
[23] He is not a king, but his descendants will be.
[24] Cryptic. They tell incomplete and half-truths.
[25] Macbeth's father. His death gave Macbeth his title.

But how of Cawdor? The Thane of Cawdor lives[26]
A prosperous gentleman; and to be king
Stands not within the prospect of belief,
75 No more than to be Cawdor. Say from whence
You owe this strange intelligence, or why
Upon this blasted heath you stop our way
With such prophetic greeting? Speak, I charge you.

[Witches vanish.]

BANQUO.
The earth hath bubbles, as the water has,
80 And these are of them. Whither are they vanish'd?[27]

MACBETH.
Into the air; and what seem'd corporal, melted
As breath into the wind. Would they had stay'd!

BANQUO.
Were such things here as we do speak about?
Or have we eaten on the insane root[28]
85 That takes the reason prisoner?

MACBETH.
Your children shall be kings.

BANQUO.
You shall be king.

MACBETH.
And Thane of Cawdor too. Went it not so?

BANQUO.
To th'selfsame tune and words.—Who's here?

[Enter Ross and Angus.]

---

[26] He is unaware of Macdonwald's death, but they speak in half-truths.

[27] They disappeared like a vapor on the earth.

[28] A root causing insanity. Perhaps a mandrake.

ROSS.

The King hath happily receiv'd, Macbeth,
90 The news of thy success; and when he reads
Thy personal venture in the rebels' fight,
His wonders and his praises do contend
Which should be thine or his. Silenc'd with that,
In viewing o'er the rest o'th'selfsame day,
95 He finds thee in the stout Norweyan ranks,
Nothing afeard of what thyself didst make,
Strange images of death. As thick as tale
Came post with post,[29] and everyone did bear
Thy praises in his kingdom's great defense,
100 And pour'd them down before him.

ANGUS.

We are sent
To give thee from our royal master thanks;
Only to herald thee into his sight,
Not pay thee.[30]

ROSS.

And, for an earnest[31] of a greater honour,
105 He bade me, from him, call thee Thane of Cawdor;
In which addition, hail, most worthy thane,
For it is thine.

BANQUO.

What, can the devil speak true?[32]

MACBETH.

The Thane of Cawdor lives. Why do you dress me
In borrow'd robes?[33]

---

[29] As fast as can be told from messenger to messenger.

[30] His reward comes from the king, not them.

[31] Token.

[32] Referring to the Sisters and the father of lies.

[33] He does not think he is deserving to be dressed in such titles. Honor,
titles, and other characteristics are often depicted as clothing in this play.

ANGUS.

    Who was the Thane lives yet,

110   But under heavy judgement bears that life

    Which he deserves to lose. Whether he was combin'd

    With those of Norway, or did line[34] the rebel

    With hidden help and vantage, or that with both

    He labour'd in his country's wrack,[35] I know not;

115   But treasons capital,[36] confess'd and prov'd,

    Have overthrown him.

MACBETH.

    [Aside.][37] Glamis, and Thane of Cawdor:

    The greatest is behind.[38]*[To Ross and Angus.]* Thanks for your pains.

    [To Banquo.] Do you not hope your children shall be kings,

    When those that gave the Thane of Cawdor to me

120   Promis'd no less to them?

BANQUO.

    That, trusted home,[39]

    Might yet enkindle[40] you unto the crown,

    Besides the Thane of Cawdor. But 'tis strange,

    And oftentimes to win us to our harm,

    The instruments of darkness tell us truths,

125   Win us with honest trifles, to betray's

    In deepest consequence.—[41]

    Cousins,[42] a word, I pray you.

---

[34] Reinforce.

[35] Ruin.

[36] Deserving death.

[37] A remark intended for the audience to hear but not the other characters.

[38] Two prophesies fulfilled, but the greatest one is yet to come.

[39] Following that to its logical conclusion.

[40] Ignite, inspire.

[41] This is the self-fulfilling prophesy Banquo is concerned about. These evil creatures tell half-truths to win the listener's trust, but they will only betray. Their words will tempt the listener to sin.

[42] Kinsmen.

MACBETH.

    [Aside.] Two truths are told,

    As happy prologues to the swelling act

130   Of the imperial theme.⁴³—I thank you, gentlemen.—

    [Aside.] This supernatural soliciting⁴⁴

    Cannot be ill, cannot be good.⁴⁵ If ill,

    Why hath it given me earnest of success

    Commencing in a truth? I am Thane of Cawdor:

135   If good, why do I yield to that suggestion

    Whose horrid image doth unfix my hair⁴⁶

    And make my seated heart knock at my ribs

    Against the use of nature? Present fears

    Are less than horrible imaginings.⁴⁷

140   My thought, whose murder yet is but fantastical,⁴⁸

    Shakes so my single state of man⁴⁹

    That function is smother'd in surmise,⁵⁰

    And nothing is but what is not.⁵¹

BANQUO.

    Look, how our partner's rapt.

MACBETH.

145 *[Aside.]* If chance will have me king, why, chance may crown me

    Without my stir.⁵²

BANQUO.

    New honours come upon him,

---

⁴³ Where Banquo focuses on caution, Macbeth looks to what he has been "promised."

⁴⁴ Temptation.

⁴⁵ These words can't be both good and evil, or true and false.

⁴⁶ His hair stands on end. He is afraid.

⁴⁷ He doesn't understand why this unseen future is more frightening than usual and apparent fears.

⁴⁸ Psalm 7:14; Proverbs 6:16-19; James 1:14-15.

⁴⁹ Though this is theoretical, his human nature is weak.

⁵⁰ Reason is smothered by these speculations.

⁵¹ The only reality for him is what he imagines could be (what is not).

⁵² He might not have to do anything; fate may make him king.

Like our strange garments, cleave not to their mold
But with the aid of use.[53]

MACBETH.

[Aside.] Come what come may,
Time and the hour runs through the roughest day.[54]

BANQUO.
150   Worthy Macbeth, we stay upon your leisure.

MACBETH.

Give me your favour. My dull brain was wrought[55]
With things forgotten. Kind gentlemen, your pains
Are register'd where every day I turn
The leaf to read them. Let us toward the King.
155   [To Banquo.] Think upon what hath chanc'd, and at more time,
The interim having weigh'd it,[56] let us speak
Our free hearts each to other.

BANQUO.
Very gladly.

MACBETH.

Till then, enough.—Come, friends.

[Exeunt.]

---

[53] One does not become used to honor and responsibility until it is tried (worn).

[54] A couplet. Times goes on no matter the circumstances.

[55] Preoccupied, shaped.

[56] Give these revelations time to show their worth.

SCENE IV. Forres; the palace

Flourish. Enter Duncan, Malcolm, Donalbain, Lennox, and Attendants.

DUNCAN.

    Is execution done on Cawdor? Are not
    Those in commission[1] yet return'd?

MALCOLM.

    My liege,
    They are not yet come back. But I have spoke
    With one that saw him die, who did report,
5   That very frankly he confess'd his treasons,
    Implor'd your Highness' pardon, and set forth
    A deep repentance. Nothing in his life
    Became him like the leaving it. He died
    As one that had been studied in his death,
10   To throw away the dearest thing he ow'd[2]
    As 'twere a careless trifle.[3]

DUNCAN.

    There's no art
    To find the mind's construction in the face.[4]
    He was a gentleman on whom I built
    An absolute trust.

        [Enter Macbeth, Banquo, Ross, and Angus.]

    O worthiest cousin!
15   The sin of my ingratitude even now
    Was heavy on me. Thou art so far before,
    That swiftest wing of recompense is slow

---

[1] Who had the warrant to execute.

[2] Owned.

[3] He had thought long and hard about his death and welcomed it as though life were nothing, or worth the trade.

[4] There is little skill or no use in trying to understand the heart of a man by his outward appearance.

To overtake thee.[5] Would thou hadst less deserv'd,
That the proportion both of thanks and payment
20   Might have been mine![6] Only I have left to say,
More is thy due than more than all can pay.

MACBETH.
    The service and the loyalty I owe,
    In doing it, pays itself.[7] Your Highness' part
    Is to receive our duties; and our duties
25   Are to your throne and state, children and servants,
    Which do but what they should by doing everything
    Safe toward your love and honour.[8]

DUNCAN.
    Welcome hither!
    I have begun to plant thee, and will labour
    To make thee full of growing. —Noble Banquo,
30   That hast no less deserv'd, nor must be known
    No less to have done so, let me infold thee
    And hold thee to my heart.[9]

BANQUO.
    There if I grow,
    The harvest is your own.[10]

DUNCAN.
    My plenteous joys,
    Wanton[11] in fulness, seek to hide themselves
35   In drops of sorrow.—Sons, kinsmen, thanes,[12]

---

[5] Macbeth goes so far beyond his duty that any repayment is slow to make up for it.

[6] Duncan wishes Macbeth to be rewarded as much as he is worth.

[7] The reward is in the service.

[8] Consider the fourth commandment: honor your father and your mother. As children to parents are servants to the king; everything they do is to safeguard him in love and honor.

[9] To embrace as a father would his child.

[10] The king plants his people and thus reaps their success.

[11] Unrestrained.

[12] Reminiscent of "Friends, Romans, countrymen."

And you whose places are the nearest, know,
We will establish our estate upon
Our eldest, Malcolm; whom we[13] name hereafter
The Prince of Cumberland;[14] which honour must
40   Not unaccompanied invest him only,[15]
But signs of nobleness, like stars, shall shine
On all deservers.—From hence to Inverness[16],
And bind us further to you.[17]

MACBETH.
The rest is labour, which is not us'd for you:[18]
45   I'll be myself the harbinger[19], and make joyful
The hearing of my wife with your approach;
So, humbly take my leave.

DUNCAN.
My worthy Cawdor.

MACBETH.
[Aside.] The Prince of Cumberland! That is a step
On which I must fall down, or else o'erleap,[20]
50   For in my way it lies. Stars, hide your fires!
Let not light see my black and deep desires.[21]
The eye wink at the hand;[22] yet let that be,
Which the eye fears, when it is done, to see.[23] [24]

---

[13] Royal we.

[14] This title makes him the heir apparent to the throne of Scotland.

[15] Others shall receive honors too.

[16] Macbeth's castle. The River Ness runs along Inverness and flows from Loch Ness.

[17] Put me deeper in your obligation, or debt, by your hospitality.

[18] Any other action not in service to you is tediousness.

[19] Messenger.

[20] He will either have to not be king or will have to step over Malcolm. But succession is not hereditary, so he still doesn't have to interfere with fate.

[21] Proverbs 12:20, 14:30, 18:12.

[22] Let the eye close to the deeds of the hand.

[23] When it does see, let it bear a horrible sight.

[24] His aside is all in rhyme. He begins to speak like the witches as he allows himself to deeply consider their "promises."

[Exit.][25]

DUNCAN.

    True, worthy Banquo! He is full so valiant;

55   And in his commendations, I am fed;[26]

    It is a banquet to me. Let's after him,

    Whose care is gone before to bid us welcome.

    It is a peerless kinsman.

[Flourish. Exeunt.]

---

[25] Macbeth exists here and then we pick up with a conversation between Duncan and Banquo about Macbeth. Their praises seem ill-placed after Macbeth's aside.

[26] It nourishes him to hear the praises of his men.

SCENE V. Inverness: Macbeth's Castle.

Enter Macbeth's wife alone, with a letter.[1]

LADY MACBETH.

"They met me in the day of success; and I have learned by the perfect'st[2] report they have more in them than mortal knowledge.[3] When I burned in desire to question them further, they made themselves air, into which they vanished. Whiles I
5   stood rapt in the wonder of it came missives[4] from the King, who all-hailed me, 'Thane of Cawdor,' by which title, before, these Weird Sisters saluted me, and referred me to the coming on of time, with 'Hail, king that shalt be!' This have I thought good to deliver thee, my dearest partner of greatness, that thou might'st
10   not lose the dues of rejoicing, by being ignorant of what greatness is promis'd thee. Lay it to thy heart, and farewell."

Glamis thou art, and Cawdor; and shalt be
What thou art promis'd. Yet do I fear thy nature;
It is too full o'th'milk of human kindness[5]
15   To catch the nearest way. Thou wouldst be great,
Art not without ambition, but without
The illness[6] should attend it. What thou wouldst highly,
That wouldst thou holily; wouldst not play false,
And yet wouldst wrongly win. Thou'dst have, great Glamis,
20   That which cries, "Thus thou must do," if thou have it;
And that which rather thou dost fear to do,
Than wishest should be undone.[7] Hie thee hither,
That I may pour my spirits in thine ear,

---

[1] This is one of the few times in the play that Shakespeare has his characters speak in prose instead of verse.
[2] Accurate.
[3] Referring to the Sisters.
[4] Messengers.
[5] She knows Macbeth to be a thoughtful and kind man.
[6] Evil, conniving.
[7] Macbeth fears the means of getting what he wants more than he desires the end itself.

And chastise with the valour[8] of my tongue
25   All that impedes thee from the golden round,
Which fate and metaphysical aid doth seem
To have thee crown'd withal.[9]

[Enter a Messenger.]

What is your tidings?

MESSENGER.
The King comes here tonight.

LADY MACBETH.
Thou'rt mad to say it!
Is not thy master with him, who, were't so,
30   Would have inform'd for preparation?

MESSENGER.
So please you, it is true. Our thane is coming.
One of my fellows had the speed of him,
Who, almost dead for breath, had scarcely more
Than would make up his message.

LADY MACBETH.
Give him tending.
35   He brings great news.

[Exit Messenger.]

The raven[10] himself is hoarse
That croaks the fatal entrance of Duncan
Under my battlements. Come, you spirits
That tend on mortal thoughts, unsex me[11] here,

---

[8] A trait typically reserved for men.
[9] "Come to me, and I will pour venomous thoughts in you and get you the crown which fate has already given you."
[10] A bird of ill-omen, here describing the messenger who announces Duncan's imminent arrival.
[11] She asks the evil spirits to take away her kindness. Also perhaps calling back to the twisted nature of the Weird Sisters.

And fill me, from the crown to the toe, top-full
40   Of direst cruelty! Make thick[12] my blood,
Stop up th' access and passage to remorse,
That no compunctious visitings of nature
Shake my fell purpose, nor keep peace between
Th' effect and it! Come to my woman's breasts,
45   And take my milk for gall, your murd'ring ministers,
Wherever in your sightless[13] substances
You wait on nature's mischief! Come, thick night,
And pall[14] thee in the dunnest[15] smoke of hell
That my keen knife see not the wound it makes,[16]
50   Nor heaven peep through the blanket of the dark
To cry, "Hold, hold!"[17]

[Enter Macbeth.]

Great Glamis, worthy Cawdor!
Greater than both, by the all-hail hereafter![18]
Thy letters have transported me beyond
This ignorant present, and I feel now
55   The future in the instant.

MACBETH.
My dearest love,[19]
Duncan comes here tonight.

LADY MACBETH.
And when goes hence?

MACBETH.
Tomorrow, as he purposes.

---

[12] Cold blooded.

[13] Invisible.

[14] Cloak, envelope. In one sense, to drape a cloth over a coffin.

[15] A brown-gray color. Darkest.

[16] She asks for her actions to be hidden from her husband.

[17] She cries for demons and hell, and she will have it.

[18] Echoing the Sisters.

[19] Note the distinct words of affection between Macbeth and his wife.

LADY MACBETH.
    O, never
    Shall sun that morrow see!
    Your face, my thane, is as a book where men
60   May read strange matters.[20] To beguile the time,
    Look like the time; bear welcome in your eye,
    Your hand, your tongue.[21] Look like the innocent flower,
    But be the serpent under't. He that's coming
    Must be provided for; and you shall put
65   This night's great business into my dispatch,[22]
    Which shall to all our nights and days to come
    Give solely sovereign sway and masterdom.[23]

MACBETH.
    We will speak further.

LADY MACBETH.
    Only look up clear;
    To alter favour ever is to fear.
70   Leave all the rest to me.

[Exeunt.]

---

[20] Both she and Duncan notice the imperceptibility of the face.
[21] Make your face appear what your heart is not.
[22] Management.
[23] She is taking the leadership role.

SCENE VI. The same; before the castle.

Hautboys[1]. Servants of Macbeth attending.
[Enter Duncan, Malcolm, Donalbain, Banquo, Lennox, Macduff, Ross,
Angus, and Attendants.]

DUNCAN.

This castle hath a pleasant seat. The air
Nimbly and sweetly recommends itself
Unto our gentle senses.

BANQUO.

This guest of summer,
The temple-haunting martlet,[2] does approve,
5   By his loved mansionry, that the heaven's breath
Smells wooingly here. No jutty, frieze,
Buttress, nor coign of vantage, but this bird
hath made his pendant bed and procreant cradle.[3]
Where they most breed and haunt, I have observ'd
10   The air is delicate.

[Enter Lady Macbeth.]

DUNCAN.

See, see, our honour'd hostess!
The love that follows us sometime is our trouble,
Which still we thank as love.[4] Herein I teach you
How you shall bid God 'ild[5] us for your pains,
And thank us for your trouble.

---

[1] An oboe.

[2] These sparrow-like birds have made their home around Macbeth as they did around temples or churches, reminiscent of Psalm 84:3. This is a place of peace and life. In the original text, the spelling is "barlet." Perhaps these martlets are rather like the martin, here only to deceive their guests. For further discussion, refer to the commentary at the end of this book.

[3] There are no protruding walls or easy places to build a nest, yet these birds have made a point to do so.

[4] His impromptu arrival is somewhat inconvenient, but he hopes it will be taken as in love.

[5] Yield (as in to yield a harvest). He is saying that Lady Macbeth will ask God to reap from Duncan payment for arriving on short notice.

LADY MACBETH.

　　All our service,

15　In every point twice done, and then done double,

　　Were poor and single business to contend

　　Against those honours deep and broad wherewith

　　Your Majesty loads our house.[6] For those of old,

　　And the late dignities heap'd up to them,

20　We rest your hermits.[7]

DUNCAN.

　　Where's the Thane of Cawdor?

　　We cours'd[8] him at the heels, and had a purpose

　　To be his purveyor;[9] but he rides well,

　　And his great love, sharp as his spur, hath holp[10] him

　　To his home before us. Fair and noble hostess,

25　We are your guest tonight.

LADY MACBETH.

　　Your servants ever

　　Have theirs, themselves, and what is theirs, in compt,[11]

　　To make their audit at your Highness' pleasure,

　　Still to return your own.[12]

DUNCAN.

　　Give me your hand.

　　Conduct me to mine host. We love him highly,

30　And shall continue our graces towards him.

　　By your leave, hostess.

[Exeunt.]

---

[6] Said in a similar spirit as the words of Macbeth and Banquo. It is an honor to serve to the king.

[7] "In gratitude for dignities given in the past, rest here like a pilgrim."

[8] Followed.

[9] Forerunner.

[10] Helped.

[11] Account.

[12] "We are your servants; everything we have and all our servants are at your disposal." Literally, what is mine is yours. She speaks as a loyal subject, but her heart is elsewhere.

SCENE VII. The same; a courtyard.

Hautboys. Torches. Enter a sewer[1] and divers[2] servants with dishes and service, and pass over the stage. Then enter Macbeth.

MACBETH.[3]

If it were done when 'tis done, then 'twere well
It were done quickly. If th'assassination
Could trammel up[4] the consequence, and catch
With his surcease[5] success[6]—that but this blow
5   Might be the be-all and the end-all—here,[7]
But here, upon this bank and shoal of time,
We'd jump[8] the life to come. But in these cases
We still have judgement[9] here, that we but teach[10]
Bloody instructions, which being taught, return
10   To plague th'inventor.[11] This even-handed justice
Commends th'ingredience of our poison'd chalice
To our own lips.[12] He's here in double trust:
First, as I am his kinsman and his subject,
Strong both against the deed; then, as his host,[13]
15   Who should against his murderer shut the door,

---

[1] Butler.

[2] Diverse, various.

[3] The following lines are a soliloquy.

[4] Tangle in a net.

[5] Cessation.

[6] What follows.

[7] In this life, on earth.

[8] Endanger.

[9] Sheol.

[10] School. In the previous lines, Macbeth uses the word "shoal." In the first folio, this is spelled "schoole" and is etymologically related to school when referring to fish. However, in Elizabethan English, the audience would have only been listening, so this word would have sounded very similar to both "school" and "sheol." So, though the words are different, there are double meanings present in the text.

[11] What comes around goes around. Psalm 7:15-16.

[12] Justice gives the mixture of our evil to ourselves to drink.

[13] Three good reasons, or witnesses, for him not to act.

Not bear the knife myself.[14] Besides, this Duncan
Hath borne his faculties so meek, hath been
So clear in his great office, that his virtues[15]
Will plead like angels, trumpet-tongued, against
20   The deep damnation of his taking-off;[16]
And Pity, like a naked new-born babe,
Striding the blast, or heaven's cherubin, hors'd
Upon the sightless couriers of the air,
Shall blow the horrid deed in every eye,[17]
25   That tears shall drown the wind.[18] I have no spur
To prick the sides of my intent,[19] but only
Vaulting ambition, which o'erleaps itself[20]
And falls on th'other—

[Enter Lady Macbeth.][21]

How now! What news?

LADY MACBETH.
30   He has almost supp'd. Why have you left the chamber?

MACBETH.
Hath he ask'd for me?

LADY MACBETH.
Know you not he has?

---

[14] As part of the host-guest relationship, there is a certain bond of trust. Among the various rules, assuming safety from harm is one. To violate this relationship in any degree was considered to be a great offense.
[15] He is such a great man and king that nothing warrants his death.
[16] Murder.
[17] Pity, like a cherub on a trumpet blast, traveling like a horse on the wind, shall proclaim the injustice to all.
[18] The rain would stop the wind.
[19] There is no good reason to act.
[20] As one might jump over a pommel horse onto the other side. Murdering Duncan will cause Macbeth to fall. But his thought is interrupted.
[21] She is the spur.

MACBETH.

We will proceed no further in this business.[22]
He hath honour'd me of late; and I have bought
Golden opinions from all sorts of people,[23]
35   Which would[24] be worn now in their newest gloss,
Not cast aside so soon.

LADY MACBETH.

Was the hope drunk
Wherein you dress'd yourself?[25] Hath it slept since?
And wakes it now, to look so green and pale
At what it did so freely? From this time
40   Such I account thy love. Art thou afeard
To be the same in thine own act and valour
As thou art in desire? Wouldst thou have that
Which thou esteem'st the ornament of life,[26]
And live a coward in thine own esteem,
45   Letting "I dare not" wait upon "I would,"[27]
Like the poor cat i'th'adage?[28]

MACBETH.

Prithee,[29] peace!
I dare do all that may become[30] a man;
Who dares do more is none.[31]

LADY MACBETH.

What beast was't, then,
That made you break this enterprise to me?
50   When you durst do it, then you were a man;

---

[22] Macbeth has made up his mind to be content.
[23] Acquired honors, specifically from this recent battle.
[24] Ought to.
[25] Once again, character is depicted as clothing.
[26] The crown; a life without risk.
[27] He is letting his duty (ought to) outweigh a daring deed for betterment.
[28] A cat that wants a fish but will not wet its paws.
[29] Please. Literally: I pray you.
[30] Befitting; make.
[31] To go outside the duties of a man, to act selfishly, is to unbecome a man.

And, to be more than what you were, you would
Be so much more the man.[32] Nor time nor place
Did then adhere, and yet you would make both.[33]
They have made themselves, and that their fitness now
55   Does unmake you.[34] I have given suck and know
How tender 'tis to love the babe that milks me;
I would, while it was smiling in my face,
Have pluck'd my nipple from his boneless gums
And dash'd the brains out, had I so sworn as you
60   Have done to this.[35]

MACBETH.
    If we should fail?[36]

LADY MACBETH.
    We fail?
But screw your courage to the sticking-place,[37]
And we'll not fail.[38] When Duncan is asleep—
Whereto the rather shall his day's hard journey
Soundly invite him—his two chamberlains
65   Will I with wine and wassail so convince[39]
That memory, the warder of the brain,
Shall be a fume, and the receipt of reason
A limbeck only.[40] When in swinish sleep

---

[32] She, in wishing to be unsexed, has become the worst of womanliness and manliness. She now encourages him to do the same.

[33] Neither time nor place were right, but he had been willing to make them happen.

[34] Now that they have presented themselves, she said he has been "unmade," playing off his statement that this is unbecoming a man.

[35] The surest sign that she has been unmade as a woman. Not only has she usurped Macbeth, but she also now states that she would destroy her child.

[36] His determination cracks, and he shows a deeper weakness: He fears getting caught more than the damnable act itself.

[37] The notch of a bow. He has pulled it back but won't let go.

[38] She has thought the whole plan out.

[39] Get them drunk.

[40] The analogy derives from a poor understanding of the body. Here, she says the wine will overpower the back part of the brain (memory) which

Their drenchéd natures lie as in a death,[41]
70   What cannot you and I perform upon
Th' unguarded Duncan? What not put upon
His spongy[42] officers, who shall bear the guilt
Of our great quell?[43]

MACBETH.
Bring forth men-children only!
For thy undaunted mettle[44] should compose
75   Nothing but males. Will it not be receiv'd,
When we have mark'd with blood those sleepy two
Of his own chamber, and us'd their very daggers,
That they have done't?

LADY MACBETH.
Who dares receive it other,
As we shall make our griefs and clamour roar
80   Upon his death?[45]

MACBETH.
I am settled, and bend up
Each corporal agent to this terrible feat.[46]
Away, and mock the time with fairest show:
False face must hide what the false heart[47] doth know.[48]

[Exeunt.]

---

serves as the guardian of the body. It would also make the middle part of
the brain (the receptacle of reason) become nothing more than a distillery
for the fumes coming from the stomach and therefore useless.
[41] Their faculties are drowned.
[42] Drunken.
[43] Place the blame of murder on the drunk servants.
[44] Temperament, composition.
[45] Who would blame them as they profusely mourn his murder?
[46] Harness his body to her will. How sad is this twisting of their marriage!
[47] The first 'false' is as a mask; the second, unfaithfulness.
[48] A heroic couplet encompassing the scene.

ACT II
SCENE I. Inverness; inner courtyard.
Enter Banquo, and Fleance, with a torch before him.

BANQUO.
How goes the night, boy?

FLEANCE.
The moon is down; I have not heard the clock.

BANQUO.
And she goes down at twelve.

FLEANCE.
I take't, 'tis later, sir.

BANQUO.
Hold, take my sword. There's husbandry[1] in heaven;
5   Their candles are all out.[2] Take thee that too.[3]
A heavy summons lies like lead upon me,
And yet I would not sleep.[4] Merciful powers,[5]
Restrain in me the cursèd thoughts that nature
Gives way to in repose![6]

[Enter Macbeth and a Servant with a torch.]

10   Give me my sword. Who's there?

MACBETH.
A friend.

---

[1] Management.
[2] Both Macbeth and his Lady have asked for darkness to hide their actions, and now they have it. Contrasting with heaven, perhaps this is hell.
[3] His dagger.
[4] He desires to sleep, but there is a wariness about him.
[5] Angels.
[6] Unlike Lady Macbeth, Banquo asks for his selfish natural desires to be suppressed rather than his good character.

BANQUO.

What, sir, not yet at rest? The King's abed.

He hath been in unusual pleasure and

Sent forth great largess[7] to your offices.[8]

15   This diamond he greets your wife withal,[9]

By the name of most kind hostess, and shut up

In measureless content.[10]

MACBETH.

Being unprepar'd,

Our will became the servant to defect,

Which else should free have wrought.[11]

BANQUO.

20   All's well.

I dreamt last night of the three Weird Sisters:

To you they have show'd some truth.

MACBETH.

I think not of them:

Yet, when we can entreat an hour to serve,

We would spend it in some words upon that business,

25   If you would grant the time.

BANQUO.

At your kind'st leisure.

MACBETH.

If you shall cleave to my consent when 'tis,[12]

It shall make honour for you.

BANQUO.

So I lose none[13]

---

[7] Abundant gifts.

[8] Rooms for work.

[9] In addition.

[10] Went to bed happy.

[11] Because of the short notice, our desire to serve was limited.

[12] Adhere to me when the time comes.

[13] Provided that he loses no honor, or can keep a clean conscience.

In seeking to augment[14] it, but still keep
My bosom franchis'd,[15] and allegiance clear,
30   I shall be counsell'd.[16]

MACBETH.
Good repose the while!

BANQUO.
Thanks, sir. The like to you.

[Exeunt Banquo and Fleance.]

MACBETH.
Go bid thy mistress, when my drink is ready,
She strike upon the bell. Get thee to bed.

[Exit Servant.]

Is this a dagger which I see before me,[17]
35   The handle toward my hand? Come, let me clutch thee:—
I have thee not, and yet I see thee still.
Art thou not, fatal[18] vision, sensible[19]
To feeling as to sight? Or art thou but
A dagger of the mind,[20] a false creation,
40   Proceeding from the heat-oppressèd[21] brain?
I see thee yet, in form as palpable
As this which now I draw.
Thou marshall'st me the way that I was going,
And such an instrument I was to use.
45   Mine eyes are made the fools o' the other senses,

---

[14] Increase.
[15] Keep his heart free.
[16] Advised.
[17] Like before, Macbeth envisions all his actions beforehand. But here he seems to have an actual vision.
[18] Ominous, foretelling death.
[19] Perceived by senses.
[20] Perhaps a double meaning: Both the vision before him and what this action will do to his mind and conscience.
[21] Fevered.

Or else worth all the rest.[22] I see thee still,
And on thy blade and dudgeon,[23] gouts of blood,
Which was not so before.[24] There's no such thing.
It is the bloody business which informs
50   Thus to mine eyes.[25] Now o'er the one half-world
Nature seems dead, and wicked dreams abuse[26]
The curtain'd sleep.[27] Witchcraft celebrates
Pale Hecate's off'rings,[28] and wither'd Murder,[29]
Alarum'd by his sentinel, the wolf,[30]
55   Whose howl's his watch, thus with his stealthy pace,
With Tarquin's ravishing strides,[31] towards his design
Moves like a ghost.[32] Thou sure and firm-set earth,
Hear not my steps, which way they walk, for fear
Thy very stones prate of my whereabout,
60   And take the present horror from the time,
Which now suits with it.[33] Whiles I threat, he lives.[34]
Words to the heat of deeds too cold breath gives.[35]

[A bell rings.]

---

[22] Either his eyesight isn't working, or it is the only part of him that is.
[23] Hilt.
[24] The vision-dagger is bleeding now.
[25] It is not real, but the reality of what he is doing now composes the image.
[26] Deceive.
[27] This is the witching hour.
[28] The goddess of night and witchcraft, pale for the moon.
[29] Shriveled Death.
[30] Brought to action by the wolf.
[31] A Roman king, mentioned in several of Shakespeare's plays, and most notably in the poem *The Rape of Lucrece.*
[32] Macbeth seems to be describing first the dagger, then symbols of evil and death, but finally seems to almost be envisioning himself as he stalks Duncan.
[33] The stones will echo his deeds beyond the evil hour of its occurrence.
[34] This is still yet talk; he hasn't done the deed.
[35] Words do not make action. Literally: talk is cheap.

I go, and it is done. The bell invites me.[36]
Hear it not, Duncan, for it is a knell[37]
65   That summons thee to heaven or to hell.[38, 39]

[Exit.]

---

[36] A bell's tolling often marked hours for prayer. Here, it marks death. The word toll means a drawn out sound, but comes from *tollen* or *betyllan*, "to lure." Where the bell might lead people to heaven, here it lures at least Macbeth to hell.

[37] The sound made by a bell. Old English: *cnyll*. Welsh: *cnull* "death bell." The Old English *cnyllan* also meant "to strike," so one might also think of a death knell.

[38] A couplet for sure, but not quite a heroic couplet as there is enjambment—that is, the thought and sentence continue from one line to the next.

[39] I am reminded of this quote by Donne, written the year after the first Folio was published: "...any man's death diminishes me, because I am involved in mankind, and therefore never send to know for whom the bell tolls; it tolls for thee." The bell tolling marks the hour of Duncan's death. Yet in this action, Macbeth dooms himself. Additionally, there are several times this play questions where a character will go after death.

SCENE II. The same.

Enter Lady Macbeth.

LADY MACBETH.

That which hath made them drunk hath made me bold;
What hath quench'd them hath given me fire.
Hark! Peace! It was the owl that shriek'd,[1]
The fatal bellman,[2] which gives the stern'st good night.[3]
5   He is about it. The doors are open,
And the surfeited grooms[4] do mock their charge[5]
With snores. I have drugg'd their possets,[6]
That Death and Nature do contend about them,
Whether they live or die.[7]

[Enter Macbeth.]

MACBETH.

Who's there? What, ho!

LADY MACBETH.

10   Alack! I am afraid they have awak'd,
And 'tis not done. Th' attempt and not the deed
Confounds us.[8] Hark! I laid their daggers ready;
He could not miss 'em. Had he not resembled
My father as he slept, I had done't.[9]

---

[1] She is startled as one caught with their hands where they do not belong.

[2] The owl, functioning as one who marks time, signals darkness and death. But the owl is not only an evil omen, that "fatal bellman." It is also an ancient symbol of wisdom, possibly crying out at the injustice and folly of their actions.

[3] Announcing the last good-night.

[4] Indulged servants.

[5] They are supposed to be guarding the King, their charge.

[6] A hot nighttime drink.

[7] Shakespeare is contrasting death with the restorative power of sleep. But also, they are in a false, drunken sleep, and the Macbeth's will mark them guilty. So, death and perhaps truth are wrestling about them, with one accusing and one defending, to say whether they will live or die.

[8] To be caught in the act before it is done will ruin them.

[9] Once again comparing a king to a father.

15   My husband!¹⁰

MACBETH.
    I have done the deed. Didst thou not hear a noise?

LADY MACBETH.
    I heard the owl scream and the crickets cry.¹¹
    Did not you speak?

MACBETH.
    When?

LADY MACBETH.
    Now.

MACBETH.
    As I descended?

LADY MACBETH.
20   Ay.

MACBETH.
    Hark! Who lies i'th'second chamber?

LADY MACBETH.
    Donalbain.

MACBETH.
    This is a sorry sight.

LADY MACBETH.
    A foolish thought, to say a sorry sight.

MACBETH.
    There's one did laugh in's sleep, and one cried, "Murder!"
    That they did wake each other. I stood and heard them.
25   But they did say their prayers, and address'd them
    Again to sleep.¹²

---

¹⁰ Suddenly her respect returns.
¹¹ Both ominous indicators of death, but she brushes them off.
¹² By saying their prayers, they settled themselves back to sleep.

LADY MACBETH.
> There are two lodg'd together.

MACBETH.
> One cried, "God bless us!" and, "Amen!" the other,
> As they had seen me with these hangman's hands.[13]
> List'ning their fear, I could not say "Amen"
30   When they did say, "God bless us!"

LADY MACBETH.
> Consider it not so deeply.

MACBETH.
> But wherefore could not I pronounce "Amen"?
> I had most need of blessing, and "Amen"
> Stuck in my throat.[14]

LADY MACBETH.
> These deeds must not be thought
35   After these ways; so, it will make us mad.

MACBETH.
> Methought I heard a voice[15] cry, "Sleep no more!
> Macbeth does murder sleep," the innocent sleep,[16]
> Sleep that knits up the ravel'd sleave[17] of care,[18]
> The death of each day's life,[19] sore labour's bath,[20]
40   Balm of hurt minds, great nature's second course,[21]
> Chief nourisher in life's feast.[22]

---

[13] As though they saw him with guilty hands.

[14] The evilness of his actions has condemned him.

[15] It appears this voice is of his mind, perhaps his conscience or a spirit.

[16] The devil lies. Where they thought they'd have peace and prosperity, they will now have fear and ruin.

[17] Tangled skein.

[18] An interesting image of a knitted garment. Here sleep untangles the messiness of life. Psalm 4:8, 139:13.

[19] Sleep is a sort of death, yet it ends the days cares.

[20] It brings healing and rest.

[21] Meals had two courses; here, sleep is the second and best.

[22] Sleep calms the mind and nurtures the soul. He killed that for himself.

LADY MACBETH.
What do you mean?

MACBETH.
Still it cried, "Sleep no more!" to all the house:
"Glamis hath murder'd sleep, and therefore Cawdor
Shall sleep no more. Macbeth shall sleep no more!"

LADY MACBETH.
45   Who was it that thus cried? Why, worthy thane,
You do unbend[23] your noble strength to think
So brainsickly of things. Go get some water,
And wash this filthy witness from your hand.[24]
Why did you bring these daggers from the place?[25]
50   They must lie there. Go carry them, and smear
The sleepy grooms with blood.

MACBETH.
I'll go no more.
I am afraid to think what I have done;
Look on't again I dare not.

LADY MACBETH.
Infirm of purpose!
Give me the daggers. The sleeping and the dead
55   Are but as pictures.[26] 'Tis the eye of childhood
That fears a painted devil.[27] If he do bleed,
I'll gild[28] the faces of the grooms withal,
For it must seem their guilt.

[Exit. Knocking within.]

---

[23] He is again likened to a bow.

[24] Evidence may be washed, but man cannot wash away his own guilt.

[25] She suddenly realizes all the physical evidence is with them, though she neglects the spiritual.

[26] Images of what once was. What gave them life is now gone.

[27] Yet she has no fear of evil, painted or otherwise.

[28] To smear with blood as with gold. Gold was considered to be a reddish color.

MACBETH.
Whence is that knocking?
How is't with me, when every noise appalls me?[29]
60   What hands are here? Ha, they pluck out mine eyes!
Will all great Neptune's[30] ocean wash this blood
Clean from my hand? No, this my hand will rather
The multitudinous seas incarnadine,[31]
Making the green one red.[32]

[Enter Lady Macbeth.]

LADY MACBETH.
65   My hands are of your color, but I shame
To wear a heart so white.[33] *[Knocking.]* I hear knocking
At the south entry. Retire we to our chamber.
A little water clears us of this deed.
How easy is it then![34] Your constancy
70   Hath left you unattended.[35] *[Knocking.]* Hark, more knocking.
Get on your nightgown, lest occasion call us
And show us to be watchers.[36] Be not lost
So poorly in your thoughts.

MACBETH.
To know my deed, 'twere best not know myself.[37] *[Knocking.]*
75   Wake Duncan with thy knocking! I would thou couldst!

[Exeunt.]

---

[29] Consider Lady Macbeth's fear of the owl's shriek in the opening lines.
[30] Invoking a pagan deity rather than the Lord.
[31] Crimson, or pinkish-red. From *incarnare*, to make flesh.
[32] His hands are so stained with blood that they would turn the seas red.
[33] She feels no guilt, yet she claims to have a woman's heart.
[34] Note this image of hands easily cleaned for later.
[35] He's so focused on himself that he forgets what's about him.
[36] Lest the right (or wrong) person find them awake and out of bed when all should be soundly asleep.
[37] To acknowledge and put aside what he has done, he denies who he is.

SCENE III. The same.

Enter a Porter. Knocking within.

PORTER.[1]

Here's a knocking indeed! If a man were porter of hell gate, he should have old turning the key.[2] *[Knocking.]* Knock, knock, knock. Who's there, i'th'name of Belzebub?[3] Here's a farmer that hanged himself on the expectation of plenty.[4] Come in time!

5   Have napkins enough about you; here you'll sweat for't.[5] *[Knocking.]* Knock, knock! Who's there, i'th'other devil's name? Faith, here's an equivocator, that could swear in both the scales against either scale,[6] who committed treason enough for God's sake, yet could not equivocate to heaven.[7] Oh, come in, equivocator.

10   *[Knocking.]* Knock, knock, knock! Who's there? Faith, here's an English tailor come hither, for stealing out of a French hose.[8] Come in, tailor. Here you may roast your goose.[9] *[Knocking.]* Knock, knock. Never at quiet! What are you?—But this place is too cold for hell. I'll devil-porter it no further.[10] I had thought to

15   have let in some of all professions that go the primrose way to th'everlasting bonfire.[11] *[Knocking.]* Anon, anon! I pray you, remember the porter.

---

[1] A gatekeeper.

[2] The gate is opened frequently because so many die. From here, he imagines himself as the porter to Hell and he is welcoming different people, and this following the scene where Macbeth could not say "Amen."

[3] A demon.

[4] A farmer hung himself in despair after hoarding goods only to be met with high supply and low prices. One might find similarities in Macbeth. He seeks only his good instead of the good of others.

[5] Have enough handkerchiefs for how much you will sweat (in Hell).

[6] A conman, or man who speaks with a double tongue. One might even picture a forked tongue in such an instance, as of the devil. James 3:6-12.

[7] This might also be referring to a contemporary court case on whether a lie was a lie if the speaker had a different meaning in mind than the hearer.

[8] Tailors would skimp on materials for clothing but charge full price. Thus, he is a deceiver.

[9] Hell is hot enough to heat his clothing iron (the goose), but the "cooked goose" also implies his plans have failed.

[10] He now returns to reality from his drunken musings to answer the door.

[11] Those who go the easy way to their own destruction.

[Enter Macduff and Lennox.]

MACDUFF.
Was it so late, friend, ere you went to bed,
That you do lie[12] so late?

PORTER.
20   Faith, sir, we were carousing till the second cock;[13] and drink, sir, is a great provoker of three things.

MACDUFF.[14]
What three things does drink especially provoke?

PORTER.
Marry,[15] sir, nose-painting,[16] sleep, and urine. Lechery,[17] sir, it provokes and unprovokes: it provokes the desire, but it takes
25   away the performance.[18] Therefore much drink may be said to be an equivocator[19] with lechery: it makes him, and it mars him; it sets him on, and it takes him off; it persuades him, and disheartens him, makes him stand to, and not stand to; in conclusion, equivocates him in a sleep, and giving him the lie, leaves
30   him.[20]

MACDUFF.
I believe drink gave thee the lie[21] last night.

---

[12] The following interaction will give many uses for the word 'lie': to deceive, to have intercourse, to make one lay down or sleep. Very often two meanings are meant for each usage of the word.
[13] The second crowing of the rooster before the sun rises. It should bring to mind Jesus' warning to Peter.
[14] Macduff: Son of Dubh/Dhuibh: dark/black (haired).
[15] An oath "by the virgin Mary."
[16] The heat of alcohol makes the nose red.
[17] Lust.
[18] Drinking arouses you, but also makes you bad at the act.
[19] A truth and untruth.
[20] The majority of this passage is a double entendre.
[21] Called him a liar/lied to him and put him to sleep.

PORTER.

That it did, sir, i'the very throat on me.[22] But I requited him for his lie, and, I think, being too strong for him, though he took up my legs sometime, yet I made a shift to cast him.[23, 24]

MACDUFF.

35   Is thy master stirring?

[Enter Macbeth.]

Our knocking has awak'd him; here he comes.

LENNOX.

Good morrow, noble sir.

MACBETH.

Good morrow, both.

MACDUFF.

Is the King stirring, worthy thane?

MACBETH.

Not yet.

MACDUFF.

He did command me to call timely on him.
40   I have almost slipp'd the hour.[25]

MACBETH.

I'll bring you to him.

MACDUFF.

I know this is a joyful trouble to you,
But yet 'tis one.[26]

---

[22] Insulted him in the deepest way.

[23] He returned the favor, though he was overpowered and unable to stand for a while, managed to cast him off (likely by vomiting).

[24] This scene up until now has been comic relief.

[25] He was asked to arrive early, but he almost lost track of time.

[26] Macduff assumes that Macbeth is joyed to have the king here but recognizes that it is still a trouble. Perhaps he perceives some disturbance on Macbeth's face, though early passages show the face to be untrustworthy.

MACBETH.
The labour we delight in physics pain.[27]
This is the door.

MACDUFF.
I'll make so bold to call.
45   For 'tis my limited service.[28]

                    [Exit Macduff.]

LENNOX.
Goes the King hence today?

MACBETH.
He does; he did appoint so.

LENNOX.
The night has been unruly. Where we lay,
Our chimneys were blown down, and, as they say,
50   Lamentings heard i'th'air, strange screams of death,
And prophesying with accents terrible[29]
Of dire combustion[30] and confus'd events,
New hatch'd to the woeful[31] time.[32] The obscure bird[33]
Clamour'd the livelong night. Some say the earth
55   Was feverous and did shake.[34]

---

[27] When we enjoy the world, it cures the pain or trouble it causes.

[28] This is what he is appointed to do. Again, everyone is very keen on service and what is required of them.

[29] Terrifying words.

[30] Literally, a burning. Perhaps referring to how terrible the subsequent events will be or to remind the listener of the recent discussion on hell.

[31] Born for affliction. And perhaps should be connected to the following owl, as this is a terrible event hatched as from an egg.

[32] Fitting for the time. This play is full of superstitious events occurring as a result of evil doings.

[33] The owl. It is a darkened, hidden bird, but also evil and portending evil tidings.

[34] Such evil done on what just a few short scenes ago was nearly described as holy ground.

MACBETH.
'Twas a rough night.[35]

LENNOX.
My young remembrance cannot parallel
A fellow to it.

[Enter Macduff.]

MACDUFF.
O, horror, horror, horror!
Tongue nor heart cannot conceive nor name thee!

MACBETH, LENNOX.
What's the matter?

MACDUFF.
60   Confusion now hath made his masterpiece!
Most sacrilegious murder hath broke ope[36]
The Lord's anointed temple, and stole thence
The life o'th'building.[37]

MACBETH.
What is't you say? The life?[38]

LENNOX.
Mean you his majesty?

MACDUFF.
65   Approach the chamber, and destroy your sight
With a new Gorgon.[39] Do not bid me speak.
See, and then speak yourselves.

---

[35] An understatement.
[36] Open, not the Midwest interjection.
[37] The phrasing is reminiscent of what is found in Scripture, but here it is again referring to how Duncan thought this place resembled a temple and now this place of life is full of death.
[38] Macbeth feels its absence.
[39] A creature that turned those who looked on it to stone (such as Medusa).

[Exeunt Macbeth and Lennox.]

Awake, awake!
Ring the alarum bell. Murder and treason!
Banquo and Donalbain! Malcolm! Awake!
70   Shake off this downy[40] sleep, death's counterfeit,
And look on death itself! Up, up, and see
The great doom's[41] image! Malcolm, Banquo,
As from your graves rise up,[42] and walk like sprites
To countenance[43] this horror!

[Bell rings.]

[Enter Lady Macbeth.]

LADY MACBETH.
What's the business,
75   That such a hideous trumpet calls[44] to parley
The sleepers of the house? Speak, speak!

MACDUFF.
O gentle lady,
'Tis not for you to hear what I can speak:
The repetition, in a woman's ear,
Would murder as it fell.[45]

[Enter Banquo.]

O Banquo, Banquo!
80   Our royal master's murder'd!

LADY MACBETH.
Woe, alas!
What, in our house?

---

[40] Unsubstantial, as opposed to Duncan's sleep in death.
[41] Judgement day. A person's death is a foreshadowing of that day.
[42] Those on the last day shall rise.
[43] To look upon, witness.
[44] Evocative of the last trumpet blast.
[45] Dramatic irony.

BANQUO.
Too cruel anywhere.
Dear Duff, I pr'ythee, contradict thyself,
And say it is not so.

[Enter Macbeth, Lennox, and Ross.]

MACBETH.
Had I but died an hour before this chance,
85   I had liv'd a blessèd time; for from this instant
There's nothing serious in mortality.[46]
All is but toys.[47] Renown and grace is dead,
The wine of life is drawn, and the mere lees
Is left this vault to brag of.[48]

[Enter Malcolm and Donalbain.]

DONALBAIN.
90   What is amiss?

MACBETH.
You are, and do not know't.[49]
The spring, the head, the fountain of your blood[50]
Is stopp'd; the very source of it is stopp'd.

MACDUFF.
Your royal father's murder'd.

MALCOLM.
O, by whom?

LENNOX.
Those of his chamber, as it seem'd, had done't.

---

[46] Nothing worthwhile in life.

[47] Everything one does is frivolous. Ecclesiastes 4:4.

[48] Only the dregs of joy, life, and the earth are left to speak of.

[49] Donalbain is out of order. It is a bit of irony as he does not know his father is dead. Where is he now in line for succession (order)? He will also grieve and be amiss emotionally.

[50] A beautiful image for us to consider in our parents.

95   Their hands and faces were all badg'd[51] with blood;
     So were their daggers, which unwip'd we found
     Upon their pillows. They star'd, and were distracted;[52]
     No man's life was to be trusted with them.

MACBETH.
     O, yet I do repent me of my fury,
100 That I did kill them.

MACDUFF.
     Wherefore did you so?

MACBETH.
     Who can be wise, amaz'd[53], temperate, and furious,
     Loyal and neutral, in a moment?[54] No man.
     Th'expedition[55] of my violent love
     Outrun the pauser, reason.[56] Here lay Duncan,
105 His silver[57] skin lac'd with his golden[58] blood,
     And his gash'd stabs look'd like a breach in nature
     For ruin's wasteful entrance;[59] there, the murderers,
     Steep'd in the colours[60] of their trade, their daggers
     Unmannerly breech'd[61] with gore. Who could refrain,

---

[51] Marked as with a badge.

[52] They were confused upon their waking.

[53] Bewildered.

[54] He provides contrary emotions to show his heart's confusion. But he, like the porter's guests, is a deceiver. His words are logical; they all probably feel the same way. But his words are merely a mask to his actions.

[55] Haste.

[56] Here is truth, but there is a double meaning: He loved Duncan, but his violence and perhaps love for his wife outran reason, which would have made him pause.

[57] Perhaps white.

[58] As mentioned before, gold was considered a rose-red color. So here we have two precious metals describing Duncan and given the stark image of red against white.

[59] He transitions to military images.

[60] Perhaps meaning sigil or flag, which here is described as murder (their trade) and Duncan's blood.

[61] As if wearing clothes. Perhaps also playing on "breached," as in their daggers which were to protect were broken by "unmannerly" murder.

56

110   That had a heart to love, and in that heart
       Courage to make's love known?[62]

LADY MACBETH.
       Help me hence, ho!

MACDUFF.
       Look to the lady.

MALCOLM. [Aside to Donalbain.]
       Why do we hold our tongues,
       That most may claim this argument for ours?[63]

DONALBAIN. [Aside to Malcolm.]
       What should be spoken here, where our fate,
115   Hid in an auger hole,[64] may rush, and seize us?[65]
       Let's away. Our tears are not yet brew'd.[66]

MALCOLM. [Aside to Donalbain.]
       Nor our strong sorrow upon the foot of motion.[67]

BANQUO.
       Look to the lady.

            [Lady Macbeth is heled off stage.]

       And when we have our naked frailties[68] hid,
120   That suffer in exposure, let us meet
       And question this most bloody piece of work
       To know it further. Fears and scruples[69] shake us.
       In the great hand of God I stand, and thence
       Against the undivulg'd pretense I fight

---

[62] He paints an emotive picture to convince his listeners of his action.
[63] "Why are we being quiet when this matter means the most to us?"
[64] A hiding place, perhaps an ambush.
[65] "What is there to say when danger may strike at any moment?"
[66] The time to weep will come.
[67] Responding to his brother, their sorrow will turn to action.
[68] Fragile mortality. Also, once they have composed themselves.
[69] Suspicions.

125   Of treasonous malice.[70]

MACDUFF.
    And so do I.

ALL.
    So all.

MACBETH.
    Let's briefly put on manly readiness,[71]
    And meet i'th'hall together.

ALL.
    Well contented.

                    [Exeunt all but Malcolm and Donalbain.]

MALCOLM.
    What will you do? Let's not consort[72] with them.
    To show an unfelt sorrow is an office
130   Which the false man does easy.[73] I'll to England.

DONALBAIN.
    To Ireland, I. Our separated fortune
    Shall keep us both the safer. Where we are,
    There's daggers in men's smiles;[74] the nea'er in blood,
    The nearer bloody.[75]

MALCOLM.
    This murderous shaft that's shot
135   Hath not yet lighted,[76] and our safest way

---

[70] With the help of God, and without deception/posturing, he will repay this uncalled for violence/treason.

[71] Armor, courage.

[72] Associate, speak with.

[73] It's easy for a liar or actor to put on a convincing face.

[74] The thanes' smiles are false and likely invite betrayal. There is no one the brothers can trust.

[75] Those closest to them are those most likely to murder them.

[76] The arrow that has brought murder and treason has not landed or found its last mark.

Is to avoid the aim.[77] Therefore to horse;
And let us not be dainty[78] of leave-taking,
But shift away.[79] There's warrant in that theft
Which steals itself when there's no mercy left.[80]

[Exeunt.]

---

[77] The best way to stay safe is to keep out of sight.
[78] Ceremonious, slow.
[79] Disappear without notice.
[80] There is authority/safety in keeping oneself away when only cruelty remains.

SCENE IV. Outside the castle.

Enter Ross with an Old Man.

OLD MAN.[1]

    Threescore and ten I can remember well,
    Within the volume of which time I have seen
    Hours dreadful and things strange, but this sore night
    Hath trifled[2] former knowings.[3]

ROSS.

    Ha, good father,[4]
5   Thou see'st the heavens, as troubled with man's act,
    Threatens his bloody stage.[5] By th'clock 'tis day,
    And yet dark night strangles the traveling lamp.[6]
    Is't night's predominance or the day's shame[7]
    That darkness does the face of earth entomb
10   When living light should kiss it?

OLD MAN.

    'Tis unnatural,
    Even like the deed that's done. On Tuesday last,
    A falcon, towering[8] in her pride of place,
    Was by a mousing owl hawk'd at and kill'd.[9]

---

[1] Unlike the witches, the Old Man tells of what has been. He is stability and tradition; whereas, they are uncertainty and superstition.

[2] Treat lightly, cheat, mock. These new occurrences make light of all that has happened before.

[3] In the seventy years he can remember, he has seen many dreadful things. But never has he encountered so terrible a night.

[4] This is not his actual father, but such a title is a sign of respect, as it was for the thanes to the king. Here, Ross asks and elder for wisdom.

[5] Here there is a double meaning: The character speaks of an eclipse, but the ceiling over the stage of the Globe Theatre was called the heavens because of its decoration.

[6] It is daytime, but the moon has covered the sun.

[7] "Is it evil prevailing or shame for what happens in the night?"

[8] Circling upward.

[9] An owl has killed a falcon, an odd occurrence. Here, Macbeth has become the owl, a creature of night.

ROSS.
And Duncan's horses—a thing most strange and certain—
15   Beauteous and swift, the minions[10] of their race,
Turn'd wild in nature, broke their stalls, flung out,
Contending 'gainst obedience, as they would make
War with mankind.[11]

OLD MAN.
'Tis said they ate each other.

ROSS.
They did so, to th'amazement of mine eyes,
20   That look'd upon't.

[Enter Macduff.]

Here comes the good Macduff.
How goes the world, sir, now?

MACDUFF.
Why, see you not?[12]

ROSS.
Is't known who did this more than bloody deed?

MACDUFF.
Those that Macbeth hath slain.[13]

ROSS.
Alas, the day!
What good could they pretend?[14]

MACDUFF.
They were suborn'd.[15]

---

[10] Favorite, darling.
[11] Creatures are turning against their nature, like disobedient children.
[12] The subtle insult is amusing. "Are you blind?"
[13] Referring to the servants Macbeth killed and silenced, but for the audience, also Duncan.
[14] "For what reason would they have killed him?"
[15] Bribed, specifically for an evil purpose.

25　　Malcolm and Donalbain, the King's two sons,
　　　Are stol'n away and fled, which puts upon them
　　　Suspicion of the deed.[16]

ROSS.
　　　'Gainst nature still.
　　　Thriftless ambition, that will ravin up
　　　Thine own life's means![17] Then 'tis most like
30　　The sovereignty[18] will fall upon Macbeth.

MACDUFF.
　　　He is already nam'd and gone to Scone[19]
　　　To be invested[20].

ROSS.
　　　Where is Duncan's body?

MACDUFF.
　　　Carried to Colmekill[21],
　　　The sacred storehouse of his predecessors,
35　　And guardian of their bones.

ROSS.
　　　Will you to Scone?

MACDUFF.
　　　No, cousin, I'll to Fife.

ROSS.
　　　Well, I will thither.[22]

---

[16] Because his sons fled, they are prime suspects.

[17] Spendthrift ambition will devour the source of life (possibly implying the sons killed their father, their source of life).

[18] Kingship, authority.

[19] The ancient royal city of Scotland, specifically for coronation. Indeed, it is assumed the baked good originates here.

[20] Clothed, endowed, crowned.

[21] Icolmkill "Iona of St. Columba." Part of the Hebrides on the west side of Scotland, and where kings were buried.

[22] Go towards that place (Scone).

MACDUFF.
>Well, may you see things well done there. Adieu,
>Lest our old robes sit easier than our new![23]

ROSS.
>Farewell, father.

OLD MAN.
40   God's benison[24] go with you, and with those
>That would make good of bad, and friends of foes![25]

[Exeunt.]

---

[23] "May things go well, or else we will wish for our old circumstances."
[24] Blessing.
[25] Isaiah 5:20; Proverbs 6:16-19.

ACT III
SCENE I. Forres. The Palace.
Enter Banquo.

BANQUO.
    Thou hast it now—King, Cawdor, Glamis, all,
    As the Weird Women promis'd, and I fear
    Thou played'st[1] most foully for't.[2] Yet it was said
    It should not stand[3] in thy posterity,
5   But that myself should be the root and father
    Of many kings. If there come truth from them—
    As upon thee, Macbeth, their speeches shine—
    Why, by the verities[4] on thee made good,
    May they not be my oracles as well
10   And set me up in hope? But hush, no more.

[Sennet sounded. Enter Macbeth as King, Lady Macbeth as Queen, Lennox, Ross, Lords, and attendants.]

MACBETH.
    Here's our[5] chief guest.

LADY MACBETH.
    If he had been forgotten,
    It had been as a gap in our great feast,
    And all-thing[6] unbecoming.[7]

MACBETH.
    Tonight we hold a solemn supper, sir,
15   And I'll request your presence.

---

[1] Performed, took part in, orchestrated. Shakespeare may also be playing off the sense of being an actor.

[2] Unlike the other characters, save Macbeth's wife, Banquo has information that leads him to suspect Macbeth as the murderer.

[3] Remain.

[4] Truth.

[5] Macbeth appears to use the royal "we" frequently in this scene.

[6] In all things, or every way.

[7] Unseemly.

66

BANQUO.
　　Let your Highness
　　Command upon me, to the which my duties
　　Are with a most indissoluble tie
　　Forever knit.[8]

MACBETH.
　　Ride you this afternoon?

BANQUO.
　　Ay, my good lord.

MACBETH.
20　　We should have else desir'd your good advice,
　　Which still hath been both grave and prosperous,[9]
　　In this day's council; but we'll take tomorrow.
　　Is't far you ride?

BANQUO.
　　As far, my lord, as will fill up the time
25　　'Twixt this and supper. Go not my horse the better,
　　I must become a borrower of the night,
　　For a dark hour or twain.[10]

MACBETH.
　　Fail not our feast.

BANQUO.
　　My lord, I will not.

MACBETH.
　　We hear our bloody cousins[11] are bestow'd[12]
30　　In England and in Ireland, not confessing

---

[8] His loyalty and duty to his king are unable to be severed. Interestingly, he does not speak to Macbeth as to a father as they did with Duncan.
[9] "Which is always weighty and useful."
[10] He will go as far as he can before now and supper, unless his horse helps him father. If not, he will arrive an hour or two after sunset.
[11] The two sons of Duncan.
[12] Residing.

Their cruel parricide,[13] filling their hearers
With strange invention.[14] But of that tomorrow,
When therewithal we shall have cause of state
Craving us jointly.[15] Hie you to horse. Adieu,
35 Till you return at night. Goes Fleance with you?

BANQUO.
Ay, my good lord. Our time does call upon's.[16]

MACBETH.
I wish your horses swift and sure of foot,
And so I do commend you to their backs.
Farewell.

[Exit Banquo.]

40 Let every man be master of his time[17]
Till seven at night. To make society
The sweeter welcome, we will keep ourself[18]
Till supper time alone. While[19] then, God be with you.

[Exeunt all but Macbeth and a Servant.]

Sirrah,[20] a word with you. Attend those men
45 Our pleasure?[21]

SERVANT.
They are, my lord, without[22] the palace gate.

---

[13] When one kills a parent or relative.
[14] Macbeth claims they are spreading falsehood.
[15] Besides talking about the brothers, they will have to talk about matters of state that concern Macbeth and Banquo both.
[16] The time calls us to leave.
[17] Everyone may do as they please.
[18] He will keep to himself.
[19] Until.
[20] Used when addressing someone lower in status than the speaker.
[21] "Do those men wish to speak with me?"
[22] Outside.

MACBETH.
   Bring them before us.

                  [Exit Servant.]

   To be thus is nothing,
   But to be safely thus.[23] Our fears in Banquo
   Stick deep, and in his royalty of nature
50   Reigns that which would be fear'd.[24] 'Tis much he dares;
   And, to that dauntless[25] temper of his mind,
   He hath a wisdom that doth guide his valour
   To act in safety.[26] There is none but he
   Whose being I do fear; and under him
55   My genius[27] is rebuk'd[28], as it is said
   Mark Antony's was by Caesar[29]. He chid[30] the sisters
   When first they put the name of king upon me,
   And bade them speak to him. Then, prophet-like,
   They hail'd him father to a line of kings.
60   Upon my head they plac'd a fruitless crown,
   And put a barren sceptre in my grip,[31]
   Thence to be wrench'd with an unlineal[32] hand,
   No son of mine succeeding. If't be so,
   For Banquo's issue have I fil'd[33] my mind;
65   For them the gracious Duncan have I murder'd,[34]

---

[23] To be king is nothing if he is still unsafe.

[24] He has a noble nature that is supreme over what else Macbeth might fear; he's also been promised kingship in his descendants.

[25] Fearless.

[26] Unlike Macbeth, Banquo is wise and slow to act. Proverbs 13:16, 14:8.

[27] Guardian spirit, nature, disposition, perception.

[28] Daunted.

[29] Octavian, Julius Caesar's nephew and successor.

[30] Banquo scolded the three Sisters.

[31] It is implied that Macbeth and his lady will have no children or they will be prevented from ruling because of Banquo's children. The throne is his, but there will be no lineage.

[32] Not of his descent.

[33] Defiled.

[34] His work will be for their benefit.

Put rancours[35] in the vessel of my peace
Only for them, and mine eternal jewel[36]
Given to the common enemy of man[37]
To make them kings, the seeds of Banquo kings![38]
70   Rather than so, come fate into the list,[39]
And champion[40] me to th'utterance![41]—Who's there?

[Enter Servant with two Murderers.]

Now go to the door and stay there till we call.

[Exit Servant.]

Was it not yesterday we spoke together?

FIRST MURDERER.
     It was, so please your Highness.

MACBETH.
     Well then, now
75   Have you consider'd of my speeches? Know
That it was he in the times past which held you
So under fortune, which you thought had been
Our innocent self.[42] This I made good to you
In our last conference, pass'd in probation[43] with you
80   How you were borne in hand,[44] how cross'd, the instruments,[45]
Who wrought with them, and all things else that might
To half a soul and to a notion craz'd[46]

---

[35] Bitterness. In this case, a bitter drink full of enemies.
[36] His soul.
[37] The devil.
[38] He realizes he gave away his soul to make someone else's sons kings.
[39] Place of combat.
[40] As in a champion in single combat.
[41] To the bitter end.
[42] "It was Banquo, not me, that kept you downtrodden."
[43] Examined the evidence.
[44] Deceived.
[45] Thwarted.
[46] Even a half-wit and insane person.

Say, "Thus did Banquo."

FIRST MURDERER.
You made it known to us.

MACBETH.
I did so, and went further, which is now
85   Our point of second meeting. Do you find
Your patience so predominant in your nature,
That you can let this go? Are you so gospell'd[47]
To pray for this good man and for his issue,
Whose heavy hand hath bow'd you to the grave
90   And beggar'd yours[48] forever?

FIRST MURDERER.
We are men, my liege.

MACBETH.
Ay, in the catalogue[49] ye go[50] for men,
As hounds, and greyhounds, mongrels,[51] spaniels,[52] curs,[53]
Shoughs,[54] water-rugs,[55] and demi-wolves[56] are clept[57]
All by the name of dogs. The valu'd file[58]
95   Distinguishes the swift, the slow, the subtle,
The housekeeper,[59] the hunter, every one
According to the gift which bounteous nature
Hath in him clos'd,[60] whereby he does receive

---

[47] Pious, filled with the gospel and forgiveness.
[48] Impoverished your family.
[49] Register.
[50] Pass, look like. An interesting contrast with the Weird Sisters.
[51] Mix-breed.
[52] Spaniard, bird-dog.
[53] A vicious dog, or low-bed man.
[54] Lapdog with shaggy hair.
[55] Long-haired water dog.
[56] Wolf-dog.
[57] Called.
[58] He lists dogs in rank of most useful to barely dog at all, insulting them.
[59] Watchdog.
[60] Enclosed in him, found in his being.

71

Particular addition, from the bill
100 That writes them all alike.[61] And so of men.
Now, if you have a station in the file,
Not i'th'worst rank of manhood,[62] say't,
And I will put that business in your bosoms[63]
Whose execution takes your enemy off,
105 Grapples you to the heart and love of us,[64]
Who wear our health but sickly in his life,[65]
Which in his death were perfect.

SECOND MURDERER.
I am one, my liege,
Whom the vile blows and buffets of the world
Hath so incens'd that I am reckless what
110 I do to spite the world.[66]

FIRST MURDERER.
And I another,
So weary with disasters, tugg'd[67] with fortune,
That I would set my life on any chance,
To mend it[68] or be rid on't.

MACBETH.
Both of you
Know Banquo was your enemy.

BOTH MURDERERS.
True, my lord.

---

[61] In each breed is some particular quality that distinguishes them from the general category of "dog."

[62] If you are not in the worst station of manhood, a step above the rest.

[63] Inspire you to this deed.

[64] Wrestles them to his love, endearment. An odd mix of fighting and nurturing words.

[65] His continued living makes his own life waste away.

[66] He has endured such sufferings that he is willing to do anything. A man with nothing to lose, so he has been made to feel.

[67] Pulled about by, wrestling with.

[68] His life.

MACBETH.
115   So is he mine, and in such bloody distance,[69]
  That every minute of his being thrusts
  Against my near'st of life.[70] And though I could
  With barefac'd power[71] sweep him from my sight
  And bid my will avouch[72] it, yet I must not,
120   For certain friends that are both his and mine,
  Whose loves I may not drop, but wail his fall
  Who I myself struck down.[73] And thence it is
  That I to your assistance do make love,[74]
  Masking the business from the common eye
125   For sundry weighty reasons.

SECOND MURDERER.
  We shall, my lord,
  Perform what you command us.

FIRST MURDERER.
  Though our lives—[75]

MACBETH.
  Your spirits shine through you.[76] Within this hour at most,
  I will advise you where to plant yourselves,
  Acquaint you with the perfect spy o'th'time,
130   The moment on't,[77] for't must be done tonight,
  And something[78] from the palace; always thought
  That I require a clearness.[79] And with him—

---

[69] Enmity, or space between them as in fencing (implied in the following).
[70] Every minute he lives stabs his heart.
[71] Royal authority.
[72] Affirm, make good.
[73] Because he does not want to lose other's support, he must fake his tears.
[74] He woos their help.
[75] He interrupts them. Now that he has their vows, he cares not for the sincerity of their words. He only cares that his own hands aren't bloodied.
[76] "I can see your sincerity." He cuts them off.
[77] Provide perfect instructions.
[78] Away.
[79] In minds of everyone, Macbeth will be blameless.

To leave no rubs[80] nor botches in the work—
Fleance his son, that keeps him company,
135   Whose absence is no less material to me
Than is his father's, must embrace the fate
Of that dark hour. Resolve yourselves apart.[81]
I'll come to you anon.

BOTH MURDERERS.
We are resolv'd, my lord.

MACBETH.
I'll call upon you straight. Abide within.

[Exeunt Murderers.]

140   It is concluded. Banquo, thy soul's flight,
If it find heaven, must find it out tonight.[82]

[Exit.]

---

[80] Defects.

[81] Decide for yourselves on your own.

[82] Once again, Shakespeare's characters question what comes after death and how the state of one's soul at the time of death affects where they go after. In a way, Macbeth is basically saying, "I wonder what comes next? Good luck in finding out!"

SCENE II. The same. A room in the Palace.

Enter Lady Macbeth and a Servant.

LADY MACBETH.
    Is Banquo gone from court?

SERVANT.
    Ay, madam, but returns again tonight.

LADY MACBETH.
    Say to the King I would attend his leisure[1]
    For a few words.

SERVANT.
    Madam, I will.

[Exit.]

LADY MACBETH.
5   Naught's had, all's spent,
    Where our desire is got without content.[2]
    'Tis safer to be that which we destroy
    Than by destruction dwell in doubtful joy.[3]

[Enter Macbeth.]

    How now, my lord, why do you keep alone,
10   Of sorriest fancies[4] your companions making,
    Using those thoughts which should indeed have died
    With them they think on?[5] Things without all remedy
    Should be without regard.[6] What's done is done.

---

[1] Direct his time.

[2] What they have, which cost them everything, is worth nothing if they are discontented and anxious.

[3] It is better to be destroyed or dead than live in anxiety because of ill-gotten gain. Proverbs 1:17-19.

[4] Wretched thoughts.

[5] "Why waste mental energy on those things which should be forgotten when they were murdered?"

[6] "You shouldn't think on that which cannot be changed."

MACBETH.
    We have scorch'd the snake, not kill'd it.
15   She'll close[7] and be herself, whilst our poor malice[8]
    Remains in danger of her former tooth[9].
    But let the frame of things disjoint, both the worlds suffer,
    Ere we will eat our meal in fear, and sleep
    In the affliction of these terrible dreams
20   That shake us nightly.[10] Better be with the dead,
    Whom we, to gain our peace, have sent to peace,
    Than on the torture of the mind to lie
    In restless ecstasy.[11] Duncan is in his grave;
    After life's fitful fever he sleeps well.
25   Treason has done his worst; nor steel, nor poison,
    Malice domestic, foreign levy, nothing
    Can touch him further.[12]

LADY MACBETH.
    Come on,
    Gentle my lord, sleek[13] o'er your rugged looks.
    Be bright and jovial among your guests tonight.

MACBETH.
30   So shall I, love, and so, I pray, be you.
    Let your remembrance apply[14] to Banquo;
    Present him eminence,[15] both with eye and tongue—

---

[7] Heal.
[8] Feeble anger.
[9] Fangs once again.
[10] Heaven and earth will crumble before he will let them be consumed by fear (perhaps poisoned through food) and nightmares.
[11] "Better to be dead (with those we sent to eternal rest in order to gain happiness) than to go crazy with sleep deprivation." Here note the many comparisons of sleep and death.
[12] Their murderous treason can do nothing worse to him. While they worry about what dangers may befall them, he is where there are no worries.
[13] Smooth.
[14] Give special attention.
[15] Favor.

Unsafe the while,[16] that we
Must lave[17] our honours in these flattering streams,
35   And make our faces vizards[18] to our hearts,
Disguising what they are.

LADY MACBETH.
You must leave this.[19]

MACBETH.
O, full of scorpions is my mind, dear wife!
Thou know'st that Banquo and his Fleance lives.

LADY MACBETH.
But in them nature's copy's not eterne.[20]

MACBETH.
40   There's comfort yet; they are assailable.[21]
Then be thou jocund[22]. Ere the bat hath flown
His cloister'd flight, ere to black Hecate's summons
The shard-born[23] beetle, with his drowsy hums,
Hath rung night's yawning peal,[24] there shall be done
45   A deed of dreadful note.[25]

LADY MACBETH.
What's to be done?[26]

---

[16] Macbeth and his lady are still not safe, so they must still be flatterers to preserve the appearance of their honor.

[17] Wash.

[18] Masks.

[19] Stop talking like this (he is apprehensive, suspicious).

[20] Copyhold, meaning lease or tenure. Our lease on life is brief.

[21] Able to be killed.

[22] Happy.

[23] Hard wings, or dung.

[24] Before these signs of night, like the bat flying back to its hiding place for the witch's call, or the beetle hums its nighttime call.

[25] The call of the witch, the sound of the beetle, and the note of death.

[26] They have traded roles again. Where Lady Macbeth usurped control, he is now taking the murderous lead.

MACBETH.
Be innocent of the knowledge, dearest chuck,[27]
Till thou applaud the deed. Come, seeling[28] night,
Scarf up[29] the tender eye of pitiful[30] day,
And with thy bloody and invisible hand
50 Cancel and tear to pieces that great bond[31]
Which keeps me pale![32] Light thickens,[33]
And the crow makes wing to th'rooky wood.[34]
Good things of day begin to droop and drowse,[35]
Whiles night's black agents to their preys do rouse.[36]
55 Thou marvel'st at my words,[37] but hold thee still.
Things bad begun make strong themselves by ill.[38]
So, prythee[39], go with me.[40]

[Exeunt.]

---

[27] A term of endearment, but here, something of an insult. In a similar way to how Lady Macbeth called Macbeth less than a man for not wanting to murder Duncan, Macbeth is belittling his wife, telling her to not worry her pretty little head about the next murders. There have been many terms of endearment between these two, but this is where it is most noticeable that their marriage has become something altogether different.

[28] Eye-closing.

[29] Blindfold.

[30] Compassionate, pitying.

[31] Moral law.

[32] In a sense, he is again asking the night to cover in darkness his deeds. Here, to close his mind's eye which might otherwise convict him.

[33] Darkens.

[34] The crow and the rook are both birds of darkness, and chatterers.

[35] Good things sleep at night while evil agents are active.

[36] The owls rouse themselves to go hunt.

[37] Where she once pushed the evil deeds, she is shocked by her husband.

[38] Evil deeds are made stronger by more evil deeds. This is done both by having to make their position more secure by cutting off any possible complications and evil is corrupting so their deeds will continue to be evil. James 1:14-15; 1 Timothy 4:2; Proverbs 5:22, 11:6.

[39] Pray thee; I ask you to. A sinister statement after such a speech.

[40] This last speech by Macbeth is most eerie. It almost seems as though he has slowly fallen into a trance and begins to chant.

SCENE III. The same. A park near the Palace.

Enter three Murderers.

FIRST MURDERER.
But who did bid thee join with us?

THIRD MURDERER.
Macbeth.

SECOND MURDERER.
He needs not our mistrust, since he delivers
Our offices[1] and what we have to do
To the direction just.[2]

FIRST MURDERER.
Then stand with us.
5   The west yet glimmers with some streaks of day.
Now spurs the lated[3] traveler apace[4]
To gain the timely inn, and near approaches
The subject of our watch.[5]

THIRD MURDERER.
Hark, I hear horses.

BANQUO.
[Within.] Give us a light there, ho![6]

SECOND MURDERER.
Then 'tis he. The rest
10   That are within the note of expectation
Already are i'th'court.[7]

---

[1] Instructions, positions, employment.

[2] There's no reason to suspect him (the third murderer) since he comes with such accurate and precise directions. It appears that Macbeth hires him later to make doubly sure that the deed is done. He is there to watch the other murderers and report to Macbeth.

[3] Belated.

[4] The setting sun encourages travelers to move quickly.

[5] Banquo is almost there.

[6] Speaking to the stable hands.

[7] The other expected guests are already inside, so they won't be seen.

FIRST MURDERER.
  His horses go about.

THIRD MURDERER.
  Almost a mile; but he does usually,
  So all men do, from hence to the palace gate
  Make it their walk.[8]

  [Enter Banquo and Fleance with a torch.]

SECOND MURDERER.
15   A light, a light!

THIRD MURDERER.
  'Tis he.

FIRST MURDERER.
  Stand to't.[9]

BANQUO.
  It will be rain tonight.

FIRST MURDERER.
  Let it come down.

  [Murderers attack Banquo.]

BANQUO.
  O, treachery! Fly, good Fleance, fly, fly, fly!
20   Thou mayst revenge[10]—O slave![11]

  [He dies. Fleance escapes.]

THIRD MURDERER.
  Who did strike out the light?

---

[8] They like to leave their horses with stable hands and walk to the palace.
[9] Brace yourselves.
[10] To Fleance.
[11] To a murderer.

FIRST MURDERER.
    Was't not the way?[12]

THIRD MURDERER.
    There's but one down; the son is fled.

SECOND MURDERER.
    We have lost best half of our affair.[13]

FIRST MURDERER.
    Well, let's away and say how much is done.

[Exeunt.]

---

[12] "Was that not the thing to do?"
[13] They only got half of the deed done; the son and heir is still alive.

SCENE IV. The same. A banquet hall in the Palace.

A banquet prepared. Enter Macbeth, Lady Macbeth, Ross, Lennox, Lords and Attendants.

MACBETH.
> You know your own degrees,[1] sit down. At first
> And last,[2] the hearty welcome.

LORDS.
> Thanks to your Majesty.

MACBETH.
> Ourself[3] will mingle with society,[4]
> And play the humble host.
5 > Our hostess keeps her state,[5] but in best time,
> We will require her welcome.

LADY MACBETH.
> Pronounce it for me, sir, to all our friends,
> For my heart speaks they are welcome.

> *[Enter first Murderer to the door.]*

MACBETH.
> See, they encounter[6] thee with their hearts' thanks.
10 > Both sides are even. Here I'll sit i'th'midst.
> Be large in mirth; anon we'll drink a measure[7]
> The table round.
> *[To the murderer.]* There's blood upon thy face.

MURDERER.
> 'Tis Banquo's then.

---

[1] Ranks.

[2] Once and for all.

[3] Macbeth's character has rapidly changed from humble and patient son to haughty and harried ruler.

[4] Step down from the king's seat and go among his guests.

[5] The queen's seat at the banquet.

[6] Respond.

[7] A cup filled to the brim.

84

MACBETH.

'Tis better thee without than he within.[8]

15   Is he dispatch'd?

MURDERER.

My lord, his throat is cut. That I did for him.[9]

MACBETH.

Thou art the best o'th'cut-throats.

Yet he's good that did the like for Fleance;

If thou didst it, thou art the nonpareil.[10]

MURDERER.

20   Most royal sir, Fleance is 'scap'd.[11]

MACBETH.

Then comes my fit[12] again. I had else been perfect,

Whole as the marble, founded[13] as the rock,

As broad and general[14] as the casing[15] air.

But now I am cabin'd, cribb'd, confin'd, bound in

25   To saucy[16] doubts and fears. But Banquo's safe?[17]

MURDERER.

Ay, my good lord. Safe in a ditch he bides,[18]

With twenty trenchèd gashes on his head,

The least a death to nature.[19]

MACBETH.

Thanks for that.

---

[8] "It is better that you have it than it being in his body."

[9] How kind of the murderer!

[10] Without equal.

[11] Escaped, and specifically from death and peril.

[12] A sudden attack, perhaps of the nerves. Also, struggle.

[13] Firm, established.

[14] Unconfined, free.

[15] Closuring, covering. Perhaps meaning the firmament or atmosphere.

[16] Sharp, imprudent.

[17] I suppose that depends on your definition of "safe."

[18] Abides. Ironically, this means "to live."

[19] Even the smallest of the gashes would have killed him.

There the grown serpent lies;[20] the worm[21] that's fled
30   Hath nature that in time will venom breed,
No teeth for th'present.[22] Get thee gone. Tomorrow
We'll hear ourselves again.[23]

[Exit Murderer.]

LADY MACBETH.
My royal lord,
You do not give the cheer.[24] The feast is sold
That is not often vouch'd, while 'tis a-making,
35   'Tis given with welcome.[25] To feed were best at home;[26]
From thence the sauce to meat is ceremony;[27]
Meeting[28] were bare without it.[29]

[Enter the Ghost of Banquo, and sits in Macbeth's place.]

MACBETH.
Sweet remembrancer![30]
Now, good digestion wait on appetite,
And health on both![31]

LENNOX.
May't please your Highness sit?

---

[20] Banquo is dead.
[21] A small serpent.
[22] Fleance is young and harmless, for now.
[23] "I will talk with you tomorrow."
[24] "You're not being very entertaining." He's a bad host.
[25] The guests will feel as though they have bought their meal if they are not repeatedly made to feel welcomed during the meal.
[26] If one was just to eat, it would be better to do so at home. But this is a feast, a celebration.
[27] The spice of a feast is ceremony, politeness, engagement.
[28] Playing on the word "meat."
[29] Without ceremony, the "meat" of the feast would be unadorned, stifled, boring.
[30] "Thank you for reminding me." (To Lady Macbeth)
[31] "Digestion needs a good appetite, and good health needs both." Also, probably a toast.

MACBETH.

40   Here had we now our country's honour roof'd,[32]
Were the grac'd[33] person of our Banquo present,
Who may I rather challenge for unkindness
Than pity for mischance.[34]

ROSS.

His absence, sir,
Lays blame upon his promise.[35] Please't your Highness
45   To grace us with your royal company?

MACBETH.
The table's full.

LENNOX.
Here is a place reserv'd, sir.[36]

MACBETH.
Where?

LENNOX.
Here, my good lord. What is't that moves[37] your Highness?

MACBETH.
Which of you have done this?

LORDS.
What, my good lord?

MACBETH.
50   Thou canst not say I did it. Never shake
Thy gory locks at me.[38]

---

[32] All of Scotland's nobility except for Banquo is under one roof.

[33] Favored, virtuous.

[34] Scold for negligence for his absence rather than pity him because something bad happened.

[35] He has broken his promise.

[36] Banquo sits in the king's chair. Though he was never promised it, his son was. Thus, there is a certain irony to him sitting there.

[37] Provokes, stirs up.

[38] Speaking to Banquo's ghost.

ROSS.
 Gentlemen, rise. His Highness is not well.

 [The Lords Begin to Rise.]

LADY MACBETH.
 Sit, worthy friends. My lord is often thus,
 And hath been from his youth.[39] Pray you, keep seat.
55 The fit is momentary; upon a thought[40]
 He will again be well. If much you note him,
 You shall offend him[41] and extend his passion.
 Feed, and regard him not. *[To Macbeth.]* Are you a man?[42]

MACBETH.
 Ay, and a bold one, that dare look on that
60 Which might appall[43] the devil.

LADY MACBETH.
 O proper stuff![44]
 This is the very painting of your fear.[45]
 This is the air-drawn[46] dagger which you said
 Led you to Duncan. Oh, these flaws[47] and starts,
 Impostors to true fear, would well become
65 A woman's story[48] at a winter's fire,
 Authoris'd by her grandam.[49] Shame itself!
 Why do you make such faces? When all's done,

---

[39] Lady Macbeth's cover for her husband is very odd. Instead of saying he's just having a moment, she is essentially saying that he's been somewhat insane since he was a child.

[40] In a moment.

[41] Make it worse.

[42] Her feistiness is back. She is both asking if he is himself again and if he has recovered his manliness.

[43] Frighten.

[44] Nonsense.

[45] Hallucinations from fear.

[46] Floating, insubstantial.

[47] Gusts, outbursts.

[48] Once again calling him unmanly while she takes on his mantle.

[49] Authorized, made certain, made up by her grandmother.

You look but on a stool.[50]

MACBETH.
Prythee, see there!
Behold, look! Lo, how say you?
70   [To Banquo.] Why, what care I?[51] If thou canst nod, speak too.
If charnel houses[52] and our graves must send
Those that we bury back, our monuments
Shall be the maws of kites.[53]

[Exit Ghost.]

LADY MACBETH.
What, quite unmann'd in folly?

MACBETH.
75   If I stand here, I saw him.

LADY MACBETH.
Fie,[54] for shame!

MACBETH.
Blood hath been shed ere now, i'th' olden time,
Ere humane statute purg'd the gentle weal;[55, 56]
Ay, and since too, murders have been perform'd
Too terrible for the ear.[57] The time has been
80   That, when the brains were out, the man would die,[58]
And there an end; but now they rise again,

---

[50] When he recovers himself, he will see it is just a chair.

[51] Macbeth senses that Banquo has communicated something more to him but didn't say anything.

[52] A place for dead bodies.

[53] If the places we put the dead won't hold them, they will be eaten by birds of prey. But also, our monuments, or legacy, will be in the bellies of birds. Our flesh does not outlast us, and perhaps maybe not even our deeds.

[54] An exclamation or interjection of disapproval. "Improper."

[55] Well-fare.

[56] Before laws were written, blood was frequently spilled.

[57] Since then, there have still been murders too awful to hear.

[58] It used to be that when you killed a man, he died.

With twenty mortal murders[59] on their crowns,[60]
And push us from our stools.[61] This is more strange
Than such a murder is.

LADY MACBETH.
　My worthy lord,
85　Your noble friends do lack you.

MACBETH.
　I do forget.
　Do not muse at me, my most worthy friends.
　I have a strange infirmity,[62] which is nothing
　To those that know me. Come, love and health to all.
　Then I'll sit down. Give me some wine, fill full.

[Enter Ghost.]

90　I drink to the general joy o'th'whole table,
　And to our dear friend Banquo, whom we miss.
　Would he were here! To all, and him, we thirst,
　And all to all.

LORDS.
　Our duties and the pledge.

MACBETH.
　Avaunt,[63] and quit my sight! Let the earth hide thee!
95　Thy bones are marrowless, thy blood is cold;
　Thou hast no speculation[64] in those eyes
　Which thou dost glare with!

LADY MACBETH.
　Think of this, good peers,

---

[59] Deadly wounds.
[60] Head, but perhaps playing on Banquo's kingly nature and his son's fate.
[61] Knock to the ground; remove from kingship.
[62] That's one word for guilt, I suppose. And how amusing that he is fine with accepting the charge of long-term insanity.
[63] Begone.
[64] Sight.

But as a thing of custom. 'Tis no other;
Only it spoils the pleasure of the time.[65]

MACBETH.
100 What man dare, I dare.[66]
Approach thou like the rugged Russian bear,
The arm'd rhinoceros, or th'Hyrcan[67] tiger;
Take any shape but that,[68] and my firm nerves
Shall never tremble. Or be alive again,
105 And dare me to the desert with thy sword.
If trembling I inhabit then, protest me
The baby of a girl.[69] Hence, horrible shadow![70]
Unreal mock'ry,[71] hence!

[Exit Ghost.]

Why, so; being gone,
I am a man again. Pray you, sit still.

LADY MACBETH.
110 You have displaced the mirth, broke the good meeting
With most admir'd[72] disorder.

MACBETH.
Can such things be,
And overcome us like a summer's cloud,
Without our special wonder? You make me strange
Even to the disposition that I owe,[73]
115 When now I think you can behold such sights
And keep the natural ruby of your cheeks

---

[65] Ruining the mood. She says this to Macbeth as much as everyone else.
[66] He is as brave as any man.
[67] Hyrcania, literally "wolf-land." By the Caspian Sea, perhaps of Media.
[68] As a murdered ghost.
[69] If he trembles, he can call him a baby doll.
[70] A word for a ghost, the shadow of life.
[71] A mockery or imitation of life.
[72] Wondered at.
[73] He has been made to feel as though he doesn't know himself—for he was considered to be brave, but not in the sight of death.

When mine are blanch'd with fear.[74]

ROSS.
What sights, my lord?

LADY MACBETH.
I pray you, speak not. He grows worse and worse;
Question enrages him. At once, good night.
120   Stand not upon the order of your going,[75]
But go at once.

LENNOX.
Good night, and better health
Attend his Majesty!

LADY MACBETH.
A kind good night to all!

[Exeunt Lords and Attendants.]

MACBETH.
It will have blood, they say; blood will have blood.[76]
Stones[77] have been known to move, and trees to speak;[78]
125   Augurs[79] and understood relations[80] have
By magot-pies[81] and choughs and rooks[82] brought forth

---

[74] His lady keeps the ruddy looks of a strongman, but he is white like a fearful woman.

[75] "Don't worry about rank as you leave."

[76] Violence will cause more of the same. Relatives will revenge. Matthew 26:52; Genesis 9:6. Also, it is possible that Shakespeare is drawing from the furies of the Greek plays, and specifically tragedies. Born of blood, the furies pursued with madness those who murdered their own family, disturbing the natural order. Family, and especially fathers and spouses, are central to this play, so it is fitting that Macbeth is driven somewhat insane by murdering his "father," Duncan.

[77] Perhaps gravestones.

[78] Nature will speak out against the unnatural.

[79] A person who interpreted natural signs.

[80] Those who prophesy.

[81] Magpies.

[82] Chattering birds that have been known to speak.

The secret'st man of blood.[83] What is the night?

LADY MACBETH.
Almost at odds with morning, which is which.[84]

MACBETH.
How say'st thou,[85] that Macduff denies his person[86]
130   At our great bidding?

LADY MACBETH.
Did you send to him, sir?

MACBETH.
I hear it by the way,[87] but I will send.
There's not a one of them[88] but in his house
I keep a servant fee'd.[89] I will tomorrow—
And betimes[90] I will—to the Weird Sisters.
135   More shall they speak, for now I am bent[91] to know,
By the worst means,[92] the worst.[93] For mine own good,[94]
All causes shall give way.[95] I am in blood
Stepp'd in so far that, should I wade no more,
Returning were as tedious as go o'er.[96]
140   Strange things I have in head, that will to hand,

---

[83] They reveal secret murderers. Shall they also reveal his deeds?
[84] It is difficult to tell if it is morning or night, perhaps lending image to Macbeth's mental and moral confusion.
[85] "What do you think?"
[86] Refuses to come.
[87] Indirectly.
[88] The nobles.
[89] He has paid spies to be in each of their houses.
[90] Early.
[91] Determined.
[92] He will get answers by way of the devil via a witch's prophecy.
[93] The worst outcome that may be.
[94] And yet, good does not come from evil.
[95] Nothing else matters but his own safety (a very unmanly thing to say; a man should defend those entrusted to him). He seeks his own good instead of the good of others. 1 Corinthians 10:24.
[96] He is in too deep to back out now.

Which must be acted ere they may be scann'd.[97]

LADY MACBETH.
You lack the season of all natures, sleep.

MACBETH.
Come, we'll to sleep. My strange and self-abuse
Is the initiate[98] fear that wants hard use.[99]
145   We are yet but young in deed.[100]

[Exeunt.]

---

[97] A couplet. What he imagines will direct his actions, and he will act before he has time to consider what he is doing.
[98] A novice.
[99] Another couplet. His fear and delusions are from a lack of experience of murder and conniving.
[100] They are new to a life of crime.

SCENE V. A heath.

Thunder. Enter the three Witches, meeting Hecate.

FIRST WITCH.
Why, how now, Hecate? You look angerly.

HECATE.
Have I not reason, beldams[1] as you are,[2]
Saucy[3] and overbold? How did you dare
To trade and traffic with Macbeth
5 In riddles and affairs of death,
And I, the mistress of your charms,
The close contriver of all harms,
Was never call'd to bear my part,
Or show the glory of our art?
10 And, which is worse, all you have done
Hath been but for a wayward son,
Spiteful and wrathful, who, as others do,
Loves for his own ends, not for you.[4]
But make amends now. Get you gone,
15 And at the pit of Acheron[5]
Meet me i'th'morning Thither he
Will come to know his destiny.
Your vessels and your spells provide,
Your charms, and everything beside.
20 I am for th'air. This night I'll spend
Unto a dismal[6] and a fatal end.
Great business must be wrought cre noon.
Upon the corner of the moon

---

[1] Literally, "fair woman," but came to have the sense of a grandmother, an aged woman, and here as hag.

[2] Her entire speech in in rhyming couplets.

[3] Impertinent.

[4] Macbeth is not an actual devote of their evil arts but saw in them means and opportunity.

[5] A river of the Hades.

[6] Ill-omened.

There hangs a vap'rous drop profound;[7]
25   I'll catch it ere it come to ground.
And that, distill'd by magic sleights,[8]
Shall raise such artificial sprites[9]
As by the strength of their illusion
Shall draw him on to his confusion.[10]
30   He shall spurn fate, scorn death, and bear
His hopes 'bove wisdom, grace, and fear.[11]
And you all know, security
Is mortals' chiefest enemy.

[Music and song within, "Come away, come away" etc.][12]

Hark! I am call'd. My little spirit, see,
35   Sits in a foggy cloud and stays for me.

[Exit.]

FIRST WITCH.
Come, let's make haste. She'll soon be back again.

[Exeunt.]

---

[7] Ready to drop.

[8] Meaning wisdom, prudence, or cunning.

[9] Spirits formed by magic.

[10] Disorder, overthrow, ruin.

[11] His overconfidence in himself shall be his undoing. Proverbs 3:5, 14:11-12.

[12] Possibly drawing from a contemporary playwright's piece, *The Witch.*

SCENE VI. Scotland.

Enter Lennox and another Lord.

LENNOX.

    My former speeches have but hit your thoughts,
    Which can interpret farther.[1] Only I say,
    Thing's have been strangely borne. The gracious Duncan
    Was pitied of Macbeth; marry, he was dead.[2]
5   And the right valiant Banquo walk'd too late,[3]
    Whom you may say, if't please you, Fleance kill'd,
    For Fleance fled.[4] Men must not walk too late.
    Who cannot want the thought[5] how monstrous
    It was for Malcolm and for Donalbain
10   To kill their gracious father? Damnèd fact!
    How it did grieve Macbeth! Did he not straight[6]
    In pious rage the two delinquents tear
    That were the slaves of drink and thralls[7] of sleep?
    Was not that nobly done? Ay, and wisely too;[8]
15   For 'twould have anger'd any heart alive
    To hear the men deny't. So that, I say,
    He has borne all things well;[9] and I do think,
    That had he Duncan's sons under his key[10]—
    As, and't[11] please heaven, he shall not—they should find
20   What 'twere to kill a father.[12] So should Fleance.

---

[1] "From what I've said, you can see we think alike. So, draw your own conclusions."

[2] He speaks sarcastically. Macbeth felt sorry for Duncan after he was dead.

[3] Banquo was a warrior, yet he died on a short night's walk.

[4] One could blame his son since he fled the scene, but again, Lennox is being flippant.

[5] "Who can help thinking…"

[6] Immediately.

[7] Slaves.

[8] The sarcasm is thick, yet also he shows the cunning of Macbeth.

[9] Managed events cleverly.

[10] In prison.

[11] If it.

[12] If Macbeth had them, they would know how those who kill fathers are punished. Which is ironic, since he kills fathers.

But, peace! For from broad words and 'cause he fail'd
His presence at the tyrant's feast, I hear
Macduff lives in disgrace.[13] Sir, can you tell
Where he bestows[14] himself?

LORD.

    The son of Duncan,

25 From whom this tyrant holds the due of birth,[15]
Lives in the English court and is receiv'd
Of the most pious Edward[16] with such grace
That the malevolence of Fortune nothing
Takes from his high respect.[17] Thither Macduff

30 Is gone to pray[18] the holy king upon his aid
To wake Northumberland and warlike Siward[19]
That, by the help of these—with Him above[20]
To ratify the work—we may again
Give to our tables meat, sleep to our nights,

35 Free from our feasts and banquets bloody knives,
Do faithful homage, and receive free honours,
All which we pine for now.[21] And this report
Hath so exasperate the King that he
Prepares for some attempt of war.

LENNOX.

40   Sent he to Macduff?

---

[13] Because Macduff speaks plainly/truthfully, and because he didn't show up to Macbeth's feast, he is out of favor with Macbeth.

[14] Hides.

[15] Speaking of Malcolm, the eldest son. Macbeth holds the throne without birthright.

[16] King Edward the Confessor of England.

[17] Despite his misfortunes, Malcolm is still treated with respect in England.

[18] Ask.

[19] Earl of Northumbria, the land just south of Scotland and eventually part of northern England. Also, possibly Malcolm's grandfather. His name is from Sigeweard: victorious lord/guardian.

[20] Unlike Macbeth, the other characters still call upon God's blessings.

[21] Order and peace may return.

LORD.
He did; and with an absolute "Sir, not I,"
The cloudy messenger turns me his back
And hums,[22] as who should say, "You'll rue the time
That clogs[23] me with this answer."[24]

LENNOX.
And that well might
45   Advise him to a caution, t'hold what distance
His wisdom can provide.[25] Some holy angel
Fly to the court of England, and unfold
His message ere he come, that a swift blessing
May soon return to this our suffering country
50   Under a hand accurs'd![26]

LORD.
I'll send my prayers with him.

[Exeunt.]

---

[22] "Umph." It's a rather childish image. Instead of answering, he turns his back to him with a humph.

[23] Loads, hinders.

[24] "You'll regret sending me this answer."

[25] That might keep Macduff wisely out of Scotland away from Macbeth.

[26] But someone should send him a message to quickly return with aid.

ACT IV

SCENE I. A cave. In the middle, a boiling cauldron.

Thunder. Enter the three Witches.

FIRST WITCH.
Thrice the brinded¹ cat hath mew'd.

SECOND WITCH.
Thrice, and once the hedgepig² whin'd.

THIRD WITCH.
Harpier³ cries. 'Tis time, 'tis time.

FIRST WITCH.
Round about the cauldron go;
5   In the poison'd entrails throw.
Toad,⁴ that under cold stone
Days and nights has thirty-one
Swelter'd venom sleeping got,⁵
Boil thou first i'th'charmèd pot!

ALL.
10   Double, double, toil and trouble;
Fire burn, and cauldron bubble.

SECOND WITCH.
Fillet of a fenny snake,⁶
In the cauldron boil and bake;

---

¹ Brindled. A coat of an animal with stripes and spots, typically darker and brown, looking as though it was burned by fire.
² Hedgehog. Used in medicine and supposedly witchcraft.
³ Harpy. A creature with the head and torso of a woman and the body of a bird of prey. As in the beginning of the play, all three of these creatures are witches' familiars, or evil spirits.
⁴ A creature of ill omen, a witch's familiar, a sign of the devil.
⁵ For 31 days, a toad has excreted venom while sleeping.
⁶ A snake living in the lowlands or marshes. Possibly also an herb.

Eye of newt[7] and toe of frog,[8]
15 Wool of bat and tongue of dog,
Adder's fork[9] and blind-worm's[10] sting,
Lizard's leg and howlet's[11] wing,
For a charm of powerful trouble,[12]
Like a hell-broth boil and bubble.

ALL.
20 Double, double, toil and trouble;
Fire burn, and cauldron bubble.[13]

THIRD WITCH.
Scale of dragon, tooth of wolf,
Witch's mummy, maw[14] and gulf[15]
Of the ravin'd salt-sea shark,
25 Root of hemlock[16] digg'd i'th' dark,
Liver of blaspheming Jew,
Gall[17] of goat, and slips of yew[18]
Sliver'd[19] in the moon's eclipse,

---

[7] Related to salamanders, newts were often associated with witchcraft. However, some have speculated that this is referring to an herb.

[8] The creatures mentioned from line 6-14 are those that dwell on land and water, perhaps associating them with two natures and able to pass between earth and the spiritual realm.

[9] Forked tongue.

[10] A harmless, legless, burrowing lizard.

[11] A baby owl. It is fitting that a creature of ill-omen is part of this ill-brew.

[12] Terrible fate.

[13] These two rhyming couplets placed together add understanding to each other. Trouble seems so harmless a word, yet they have doubled it, making it a terrible fate. Moreover, toil is hard work or a snare, and trouble a turbulent mind. And now we see that this fire burning and cauldron bubbling is a drink from Hell.

[14] Mouth.

[15] Belly.

[16] A poisonous plant.

[17] Bile.

[18] A tree symbolizing both death and immortality. Once considered centers of witchcraft and evil, Churches came to be planted by them and, in a small way, took on a symbolism like that of the olive tree.

[19] Broken off.

Nose of Turk,[20] and Tartar's[21] lips,
30   Finger of birth-strangled babe
       Ditch-deliver'd by a drab,[22]
       Make the gruel thick and slab.[23]
       Add thereto a tiger's chaudron[24]
       For th'ingredience of our cauldron.

ALL.
35   Double, double, toil and trouble;
       Fire burn, and cauldron bubble.[25]

SECOND WITCH.
       Cool it with a baboon's blood.
       Then the charm is firm[26] and good.[27]

                    [Enter Hecate.]

HECATE.
       O, well done! I commend your pains,
40   And everyone shall share i'th' gains.
       And now about the cauldron sing
       Like elves and fairies in a ring,[28]
       Enchanting all that you put in.

        [Music and a song: "Black Spirits," &c.][29]

                    [Exit Hecate.]

---

[20] Someone from the Ottoman Empire.

[21] A Mongolian, but this perhaps would have a double connotation to the land of Tartarus, or the underworld.

[22] Born in a ditch by a harlot.

[23] Thick and sticky.

[24] Entrails.

[25] The witches repeat in threes.

[26] Strong, permanent.

[27] Finished.

[28] A circle of mushrooms is also called a fairy ring. They were considered to be portals to another world.

[29] Song drawn from a contemporary playwright's piece, *The Witch.*

SECOND WITCH.
>　　By the pricking[30] of my thumbs,

45　Something wicked this way comes.

>　　Open, locks,

>　　Whoever knocks![31]

[Enter Macbeth.]

MACBETH.
>　　How now,[32] you secret, black, and midnight hags!

>　　What is't you do?

ALL.
>　　A deed without a name.[33]

MACBETH.

50　I conjure you, by that which you profess,

>　　Howe'er you come to know it, answer me.[34]

>　　Though you untie the winds, and let them fight

>　　Against[35] the churches,[36] though the yeasty[37] waves

>　　Confound and swallow navigation up,[38]

55　Though bladed[39] corn be lodg'd,[40] and trees blown down,

>　　Though castles topple on their warders'[41] heads,

>　　Though palaces and pyramids do slope

>　　Their heads to their foundations, though the treasure

>　　Of nature's germen[42] tumble altogether,[43]

---

[30] Tingling.

[31] She commands the door to open to whomever knocks.

[32] "What is happening?" or hello. It is most often used as a greeting.

[33] There is something profoundly eerie about this reply. It implies that it is so evil, there literally isn't a word for it.

[34] The knowledge he seeks justifies the means they use to get it.

[35] Tear down.

[36] Macbeth steps further into the demonic and away from Truth.

[37] Foamy, like proofed yeast.

[38] Essentially, send sailors to their deaths.

[39] Unripe, still in the blades or husk of the plant.

[40] Flattened.

[41] Inhabitants.

[42] Seeds, or foundational elements.

[43] Everything in nature becomes mixed.

60   Even till destruction sicken,[44] answer me
       To what I ask you.

FIRST WITCH.
    Speak.

SECOND WITCH.
    Demand.

THIRD WITCH.
    We'll answer.

FIRST WITCH.
    Say, if thou'dst rather hear it from our mouths,
    Or from our masters?

MACBETH.
    Call 'em, let me see 'em.

FIRST WITCH.
    Pour in sow's blood, that hath eaten
65 Her nine farrow;[45] grease that's sweaten
    From the murderer's gibbet[46] throw
    Into the flame.

ALL.
    Come, high or low,[47]
    Thyself and office deftly show![48]

        [Thunder. First Apparition, an armed Head.][49]

MACBETH.
    Tell me, thou unknown power,—[50]

---

[44] "Even if destruction itself is full to sickness of its own destruction."
[45] A female pig that has eaten her nine offspring.
[46] Sweat that was sweetened from a murderer on the gallows.
[47] Spirits from above or from hell.
[48] Show themselves and what they do/how they function.
[49] These apparitions foreshadow the future of Macbeth in themselves.
[50] Macbeth is still trying to deny that he is playing with hellfire.

FIRST WITCH.

He knows thy thought.

70   Hear his speech, but say thou naught.

APPARITION.

Macbeth! Macbeth! Macbeth! Beware Macduff;
Beware the Thane of Fife. Dismiss me. Enough.

[Descends.]

MACBETH.

Whate'er thou art, for thy good caution, thanks;
Thou hast harp'd[51] my fear aright. But one word more—

FIRST WITCH.

75   He will not be commanded. Here's another,
More potent than the first.

[Thunder. Second Apparition, a bloody Child.]

APPARITION.

Macbeth! Macbeth! Macbeth!

MACBETH.

Had I three ears, I'd hear thee.

APPARITION.

Be bloody, bold, and resolute; laugh to scorn
80   The power of man, for none of woman born
Shall harm Macbeth.

[Descends.]

MACBETH.

Then live, Macduff; what need I fear of thee?[52]
But yet I'll make assurance double sure,
And take a bond[53] of fate. Thou shalt not live,
85   That I may tell pale-hearted fear it lies,

---

[51] Touched with sound, as with a harp.
[52] To him, these two apparitions have contradicted each other.
[53] Guarantee.

And sleep in spite of thunder.

[Thunder. Third Apparition, a Child crowned, with a tree in his hand.][54]

What is this,
That rises like the issue of a king,
And wears upon his baby brow the round
And top of sovereignty?

ALL.
Listen, but speak not to't.

APPARITION.
90   Be lion-mettled, proud, and take no care
Who chafes, who frets, or where conspirers are.
Macbeth shall never vanquish'd be until
Great Birnam wood to high Dunsinane hill
Shall come against him.[55]

[Descends.]

MACBETH.
That will never be.
95   Who can impress the forest, bid the tree
Unfix his earth-bound root?[56] Sweet bodements,[57] good!
Rebellious head,[58] rise never till the wood[59]

---

[54] This is a son that shall rise and be king. Also, the tree is of the Birnam Wood, revealed in the apparition's following speech, where fate shall take place. Each of these apparitions contain double meanings, and thus, are double tongued. Though they speak one thing, the visions show and mean another, thus telling the truth yet leading Macbeth to destruction. Whose severed head warns of or from the future? Why a bloody child? Keep these images in mind for the final act.

[55] Macbeth is not to worry about anyone who plots against him, for no one will overthrow him until the Birnam forest itself comes against Dunsinane Hill. This hill was of a great height, and on its top was a fortress where Macbeth stayed. It is a short distance from Scone, where the palace was.

[56] He mocks this thought, as you can't tell a tree to uproot and walk away.

[57] Prophecies.

[58] Perhaps thinking of Duncan and Banquo in relation to the apparition.

[59] The image is of the prophecy and judgement day when the dead rise.

Of Birnam rise, and our[60] high-plac'd Macbeth
Shall live the lease of nature, pay his breath
100   To time and mortal custom.[61, 62] Yet my heart
Throbs to know one thing. Tell me, if your art
Can tell so much: shall Banquo's issue ever
Reign in this kingdom?

ALL.
Seek to know no more.[63]

MACBETH.
I will be satisfied. Deny me this,
105   And an eternal curse fall on you! Let me know.
Why sinks that cauldron?[64] And what noise is this?

[Cauldron Descends. Hautboys.][65]

FIRST WITCH.
Show!

SECOND WITCH.
Show!

THIRD WITCH.
Show!

ALL.
110   Show his eyes, and grieve his heart;
Come like shadows, so depart!

[A show of eight kings, and Banquo last, with a glass[66] in his hand.]

---

[60] He's returned to the royal we.

[61] Because these things cannot happen, he will use up his full life and die a natural death.

[62] After reading the words of the apparitions and Macbeth's response, consider Hecate's words in 3.5.26-33.

[63] They have answered almost everything so far, yet to tell him more will keep him safe perhaps.

[64] They were leaving. Also, there were trap doors on the stage.

[65] Instruments.

[66] A mirror.

MACBETH.

Thou are too like the spirit of Banquo.[67] Down!

Thy crown does sear mine eyeballs. And thy hair,

Thou other[68] gold-bound brow, is like the first.

115 A third is like the former. Filthy hags!

Why do you show me this? A fourth! Start, eyes!

What, will the line stretch out to th'crack of doom?

Another yet! A seventh! I'll see no more.

And yet the eighth appears, who bears a glass

120 Which shows me many more;[69] and some I see

That twofold balls[70] and treble sceptres[71] carry.

Horrible sight! Now I see 'tis true,

For the blood-bolter'd[72] Banquo smiles upon me[73]

And points at them for his. What, is this so?

[Apparitions vanish.]

FIRST WITCH.

125 Ay, sir, all this is so. But why

Stands Macbeth thus amazedly?[74]

Come, sisters, cheer we up his sprites,[75]

And show the best of our delights.

---

[67] Macbeth is seeing the kings one by one. So, he says this one looks like Banquo, not realizing at first that they are related.

[68] The second king.

[69] The mirror the eighth king holds, perhaps a magic mirror, shows many more kings to come afterwards. There is a sad irony in this tale where fathers and sons are central to the story, and crucial for life and legacy, that Macbeth has none.

[70] Probably a globus cruciger. There are two for a coronation in two places.

[71] The three scepters show that this king reigns over three countries. It is assumed that this king is supposed to represent King James I, or the VI of Scotland. His mother was Mary, Queen of Scots. He attained the throne and ruled over Scotland, Ireland, and England on the death of Elizabeth I.

[72] His hair is matted/smeared with blood.

[73] Banquo finally appears. And though he is dead, Macbeth has not changed fate.

[74] Didn't you listen to the prophecy? If only he had three ears!

[75] Spirits.

I'll charm the air to give a sound,
130   While you perform your antic round,[76]
        That this great king may kindly say
        Our duties did his welcome pay.

[Music. The Witches dance, and vanish.]

MACBETH.
        Where are they? Gone? Let this pernicious hour
        Stand aye accursèd in the calendar!
135   Come in, without there!

[Enter Lennox.]

LENNOX.
        What's your Grace's will?

MACBETH.
        Saw you the Weird Sisters?

LENNOX.
        No, my lord.

MACBETH.
        Came they not by you?

LENNOX.
        No, indeed, my lord.

MACBETH.
        Infected be the air whereon they ride,
        And damn'd all those that trust them![77] I did hear
140   The galloping of horse. Who was't came by?

LENNOX.
        'Tis two or three, my lord, that bring you word
        Macduff is fled to England.

---

[76] They are dancing crazily.

[77] He is not wrong, as he should have known before now.

MACBETH.
    Fled to England!

LENNOX.
    Ay, my good lord.

MACBETH. [Aside.]
    Time, thou anticipat'st[78] my dread exploits.
145   The flighty[79] purpose never is o'ertook
    Unless the deed go with it.[80] From this moment
    The very firstlings[81] of my heart shall be
    The firstlings of my hand.[82] And even now,
    To crown my thoughts with acts, be it thought and done:
150   The castle of Macduff I will surprise,
    Seize upon Fife, give to th'edge o'th'sword
    His wife, his babes, and all unfortunate souls[83]
    That trace him in his line.[84] No boasting like a fool;
    This deed I'll do before this purpose cool.[85]
155   But no more sights![86] —Where are these gentlemen?
    Come, bring me where they are.

[Exeunt.]

---

[78] Anticipates, thwarts.

[79] Fleeting.

[80] Unless something is done immediately, a person won't get the chance to do it. Time flies, one might say.

[81] Firstborn.

[82] As soon as his mind conceives of something, his hand will do it.

[83] Those in positions of authority are supposed to protect, and in some cases, provide for. Macbeth has become a shell of a man and a bad king by seeking the destruction of his people, his children.

[84] Everyone in his family.

[85] He will act now before he loses his nerve. Also, another evil couplet.

[86] One wonders if Macbeth is starting to have more hallucinations.

SCENE II. Fife. Macduff's Castle.

Enter Lady Macduff, her Son, and Ross.

LADY MACDUFF.
What had he done to make him fly[1] the land?

ROSS.
You must have patience, madam.

LADY MACDUFF.
He had none.
His flight was madness. When our actions do not,
Our fears do make us traitors.[2]

ROSS.
You know not
5   Whether it was his wisdom[3] or his fear.

LADY MACDUFF.
Wisdom? To leave his wife, to leave his babes,
His mansion, and his titles,[4] in a place
From whence himself does fly? He loves us not;
He wants[5] the natural touch.[6] For the poor wren,[7]
10   The most diminutive of birds, will fight,
Her young ones in her nest, against the owl.[8]
All is the fear, and nothing is the love;[9]

---

[1] This scene has the most references to birds and flight in all the play.
[2] She is not wrong. The others thought the same of Duncan's sons at first, thinking they showed guilt of killing their father by fleeing immediately.
[3] This is also true. Lady Macduff was not informed of the reason he fled the country. The Macbeth's have this over them: they, at least initially, told each other everything.
[4] Possessions from his title as a thane.
[5] Lacks.
[6] The instinct to protect.
[7] The little king bird. Small, but fierce. Read more in the commentary at the end of this book.
[8] The wren will protect her nest against predators when she has babies.
[9] A particularly heartbreaking line. Here she truly believes that her husband does not love them, is not a man. Lady Macbeth railed against her husband

As little is the wisdom, where the flight
So runs against all reason.

ROSS.

My dearest coz,[10]
15   I pray you, school[11] yourself. But, for your husband,
He is noble, wise, judicious, and best knows
The fits o'th'season.[12] I dare not speak much further,
But cruel are the times when we are traitors
And do not know ourselves,[13] when we hold rumour
20   From what we fear,[14] yet know not what we fear,
But float upon a wild and violent sea
Each way and none.[15] I take my leave of you;
Shall not be long but I'll be here again.
Things at the worst will cease, or else climb upward
25   To what they were before.[16]—My pretty cousin,
Blessing upon you!

LADY MACDUFF.

Father'd he is, and yet he's fatherless.[17]

---

and literally called him unmanly because he wouldn't kill an innocent. But here Lady Macduff truly believes her husband a coward because he left them alone (a greater sign of unmanliness). She doesn't have to say it like Lady Macbeth. It is clear enough from his actions. But though he is not a coward, how much would have been saved if they had spoken.

[10] Kinswoman. Used among nobility, but not necessarily meaning they were related. The thanes refer to each other this way as well.

[11] Control.

[12] He knows the convoluted times they are in.

[13] They have done no wrong, but suspicion and fear breeds fear and suspicion of innocents.

[14] Because they are fearful, they believe every rumor they hear.

[15] This way and that. They have no foundation, no faith.

[16] At their worst, terrible events will come to an end and won't get lower. Or things will go back to how they were before.

[17] Her son has a father, but he is still without. Fathers are crucial in this story. As with Duncan, leaders were those who were supposed to provide and protect, taking on the public form of a father. As he seemingly abdicated his duty to protect, it is as though his son has no father.

ROSS.
I am so much a fool, should I stay longer,
It would be my disgrace and your discomfort.[18]
30　　I take my leave at once.

[Exit Ross.]

LADY MACDUFF.
Sirrah,[19] your father's dead.[20]
And what will you do now? How will you live?

SON.
As birds do, mother.

LADY MACDUFF.
What, with worms and flies?

SON.
With what I get, I mean; and so do they.[21]

LADY MACDUFF.
Poor bird! Thou'dst never fear the net nor lime,[22]
35　　The pit-fall nor the gin.[23]

SON.
Why should I, mother? Poor birds they are not set for.[24]
My father is not dead, for all your saying.

LADY MACDUFF.
Yes, he is dead. How wilt thou do for a father?

---

[18] It appears he is at the point of tears. It probably pains him to see this lady in such distress and to know it is for naught, but he can't do anything.

[19] Essentially means "sir" but it was only used for young boys, or towards men if they were held in low esteem.

[20] Not literally, but for all practical purposes, he is without a father.

[21] Matthew 6:25-34.

[22] A sticky substance used to trap birds.

[23] He does not have a healthy or prudent fear of hash reality, full of snares and traps.

[24] If he is a "poor" or pitiful bird, then the traps won't be set for him but for a better bird.

116

SON.

Nay, how will you do for a husband?

LADY MACDUFF.

40   Why, I can buy me twenty at any market.[25]

SON.

Then you'll buy 'em to sell again.

LADY MACDUFF.

Thou speak'st with all thy wit,
And yet, i'faith, with wit enough for thee.[26]

SON.

Was my father a traitor, mother?

LADY MACDUFF.

45   Ay, that he was.

SON.

What is a traitor?

LADY MACDUFF.

Why, one that swears and lies.[27]

SON.

And be all traitors that do so?

LADY MACDUFF.

Every one that does so is a traitor and must be hanged.

SON.

50   And must they all be hanged that swear and lie?

---

[25] She is speaking flippantly, as though good men, or men good enough to be husbands, are common enough to be bought easily.

[26] He is speaking as a child, yet he is quite smart. The tenderness and playfulness between this mother and her son in this scene are quite touching.

[27] Perhaps not speaking so much of his fealty to his king but to abandoning his family. He promised/swore to be devoted to his wife, his children, and his position as a thane. But to her, he lied.

LADY MACDUFF.
    Every one.

SON.
    Who must hang them?

LADY MACDUFF.
    Why, the honest men.

SON.
    Then the liars and swearers are fools, for there are liars and
55   swearers enow²⁸ to beat the honest men and hang up them.²⁹

LADY MACDUFF.
    Now, God help thee, poor monkey! But how wilt thou do for a
    father?

SON.
    If he were dead, you'd weep for him; if you would not, it were a
    good sign that I should quickly have a new father.

LADY MACDUFF.
60   Poor prattler,³⁰ how thou talk'st!

                        [Enter a Messenger.]

MESSENGER.
    Bless you, fair dame! I am not to you known,
    Though in your state of honour I am perfect.³¹
    I doubt³² some danger does approach you nearly,
    If you will take a homely³³ man's advice,
65   Be not found here. Hence, with your little ones.
    To fright you thus, methinks, I am too savage;³⁴

---

²⁸ Enough.
²⁹ There are more promises-breakers than honest men, so "might should make right," so to speak.
³⁰ Babbler.
³¹ He knows full well that she is a Lady.
³² Fear.
³³ Plain, lowly.
³⁴ He feels badly for frightening her.

To do worse to you were fell cruelty,[35]
Which is too nigh your person.[36] Heaven preserve you!
I dare abide no longer.

[Exit Messenger.]

LADY MACDUFF.
Whither[37] should I fly?
70   I have done no harm.[38] But I remember now
I am in this earthly world, where to do harm
Is often laudable, to do good sometime
Accounted dangerous folly.[39] Why then, alas,
Do I put up that womanly defense
75   To say I have done no harm?

[Enter Murderers.]

What are these faces?[40]

FIRST MURDERER.
Where is your husband?

LADY MACDUFF.
I hope in no place so unsanctified[41]
Where such as thou mayst find him.

FIRST MURDERER.
He's a traitor.

---

[35] But it would be worse to say nothing.

[36] Danger will be here soon.

[37] Where.

[38] She does not see that, in some way, what her husband showed was prudence, not folly. But where he thought his family might be safe without him there, he was wrong.

[39] She begins to see the times and her husband's intent and actions.

[40] People.

[41] Disreputable, hellish. What a fantastic word for such a group as these. It harkens back to the opening scene of Macbeth's castle one described as a hallowed temple, becoming a tomb for Duncan. Such evil as these men can only come from an unholy place. Also, she is not so subtly insulting them by saying her husband can't be in so horrible a place that they would know about and be able find him.

SON.
Thou liest, thou shag-ear'd[42] villain![43]

FIRST MURDERER.
What, you egg![44]

[Stabbing him.]

80   Young fry[45] of treachery![46]

SON.
He has kill'd me, mother:
Run away, I pray you!

[Dies. Exit Lady Macduff crying "Murder!" pursued by Murderers with
the Son's body.]

---

[42] Criminals sometimes had their noses and ears cut, so their ears would look like shaggy hair. But perhaps Shakespeare just meant shaggy-haired and these men looked rough and villainous.

[43] He would listen with patience the accusations of his mother, but no stranger shall insult his father. He will defend his honor.

[44] On one hand, this is a rather curious insult. On the other, Lady Macduff has compared her family to birds, specifically a wren, and with flight. Here the murderer calls him an egg, even more defenseless than a small bird, and kills him.

[45] A small fish or child.

[46] Child of a traitor.

SCENE III. England. King Edward's Palace.

Enter Malcolm and Macduff.

MALCOLM.
Let us seek out some desolate shade and there
Weep our sad bosoms empty.

MACDUFF.
Let us rather
Hold fast the mortal[1] sword and, like good men,
Bestride[2] our down-fall'n birthdom.[3] Each new morn
5   New widows howl, new orphans cry,[4] new sorrows
Strike heaven on the face, that it resounds
As if it felt with Scotland and yell'd out
Like syllable of dolour.[5]

MALCOLM.
What I believe, I'll wail;[6]
What know, believe;[7] and what I can redress,
10   As I shall find the time to friend, I will.[8]
What you have spoke, it may be so perchance.[9]
This tyrant, whose sole name[10] blisters our tongues,
Was once thought honest. You have loved him well;
He hath not touch'd you yet.[11] I am young; but something

---

[1] Deadly, as in bringing mortality; or perhaps encouraging him to fight
with the life he has left.
[2] Stand and defend.
[3] Native land.
[4] An interesting observation considering the previous scene. This is dramatic irony to the listener or reader.
[5] Same word of pain.
[6] What he knows to be wrong, he will mourn.
[7] What he knows to be true, that he'll put his faith in.
[8] What he can correct in good time, he will fix.
[9] "What you said might be true."
[10] Merely mentioning the name.
[11] Malcolm is not a fool. Macduff was a near friend of Macbeth. And as
(he thinks) Macduff remains unharmed, it makes him a bit suspicious.

15   You may deserve of him through me,[12] and wisdom[13]
      To offer up a weak, poor, innocent lamb
      To appease an angry god.

MACDUFF.
      I am not treacherous.

MALCOLM.
      But Macbeth is.
      A good and virtuous nature may recoil[14]
20   In an imperial charge.[15, 16] But I shall crave your pardon.[17]
      That which you are, my thoughts cannot transpose;[18]
      Angels are bright still, though the brightest fell.[19]
      Though all things foul would wear the brows of grace,
      Yet grace must still look so.[20]

MACDUFF.
      I have lost my hopes.[21]

MALCOLM.
25   Perchance even there where I did find my doubts.[22]
      Why in that rawness[23] left you wife and child,

---

[12] Macduff may gain favor with Macbeth by bringing him Malcolm.

[13] The wisdom of one's actions are frequently questioned in this play. What is it to be wise? To act wisely? Is it to do what is in your own interests, or is it to do what is right? Further, what makes a man?

[14] Draw back.

[15] Be shot forth. In previous scenes, Macbeth has been likened to a bow.

[16] There is perhaps a double meaning in this statement. He is stating that Macduff's good nature may be put aside at royal command (a good nature is withdrawn when one is sent/shot forth, like a charge or bolt from a bow, by the king's command) but also that Macbeth's good nature was withdrawn upon his ascension to the throne.

[17] "Please forgive me."

[18] Whatever Malcolm may think cannot change who Macduff really is.

[19] Referring to Lucifer, the angel of "light."

[20] Though evil things can disguise themselves as good, good will also appear good as is its nature.

[21] He is trying to persuade Malcolm to fight Macbeth.

[22] Perhaps Macduff lost his hope about Malcolm where Malcolm was mistrustful of Macduff's loyalties.

[23] Currently turbulent times.

Those precious motives, those strong knots of love,
Without leave-taking? I pray you,
Let not my jealousies[24] be your dishonours,[25]
30 But mine own safeties.[26] You may be rightly just,[27]
Whatever I shall think.

MACDUFF.
Bleed, bleed, poor country!
Great tyranny, lay thou thy basis sure,
For goodness dare not check thee; [28] wear thou thy wrongs,
The title is affeer'd![29] Fare thee well, lord.
35 I would not be the villain that thou think'st
For the whole space that's in the tyrant's grasp
And the rich East to boot.[30]

MALCOLM.
Be not offended.
I speak not as in absolute fear[31] of you.
I think our country sinks beneath the yoke;
40 It weeps, it bleeds, and each new day a gash
Is added to her wounds. I think withal[32]
There would be hands uplifted in my right;[33]
And here, from gracious England, have I offer
Of goodly thousands.[34] But, for all this,
45 When I shall tread upon the tyrant's head,
Or wear it on my sword, yet my poor country

---

[24] Suspicions.

[25] Appear slanderous (of Macduff).

[26] But prudence to protect himself.

[27] Honest.

[28] He is saying that Tyranny should feel free to lay a strong foundation, for good is hesitant to put it in check.

[29] Tyranny can freely display their wrongdoing. Their position is safe.

[30] "I wouldn't be the villain you describe if I was offered everything Macbeth possesses and the riches of the East as well."

[31] Mistrust.

[32] In addition.

[33] Cause, or right to the throne.

[34] England has offered troops.

Shall have more vices than it had before,
More suffer,[35] and more sundry[36] ways than ever,
By him that shall succeed.

MACDUFF.
What should he be?[37]

MALCOLM.
50   It is myself I mean, in whom I know
All the particulars of vice so grafted[38]
That, when they shall be open'd, black Macbeth
Will seem as pure as snow, and the poor state[39]
Esteem him as a lamb, being compar'd
55   With my confineless[40] harms.

MACDUFF.
Not in the legions
Of horrid hell can come a devil more damn'd
In evils to top Macbeth.

MALCOLM.
I grant him bloody,
Luxurious, avaricious, false, deceitful,
Sudden, malicious,[41] smacking of every sin
60   That has a name. But there's no bottom, none,
In my voluptuousness.[42] Your wives, your daughters,
Your matrons, and your maids, could not fill up
The cistern of my lust, and my desire
All continent impediments would o'erbear
65   That did oppose my will.[43] Better Macbeth

---

[35] Suffer in worse.
[36] Various.
[37] "Who do you mean?"
[38] Sin has made itself one with him. What an image!
[39] Scotland.
[40] Without boundary. Another apt description of sin.
[41] Murderous, lecherous, greedy, lying, deceitful, impetuous, malicious.
[42] Desires, specifically, lust. Where Macbeth is full of every vice that has a name, Malcolm's vices are bottomless. "Deeds without names," perhaps.
[43] His desire would overpower any restraint.

Than such an one to reign.

MACDUFF.
　　Boundless intemperance
In nature is a tyranny;[44] it hath been
Th' untimely emptying of the happy throne,
And fall of many kings.[45] But fear not yet
70　To take upon you what is yours.[46] You may
Convey your pleasures in a spacious plenty,
And yet seem cold; the time you may so hoodwink.[47]
We have willing dames enough.[48] There cannot be
That vulture in you, to devour so many
75　As will to greatness dedicate themselves,
Finding it so inclin'd.[49]

MALCOLM.
　　With this there grows
In my most ill-compos'd affection[50] such
A staunchless avarice that, were I king,
I should cut off the nobles for their lands,
80　Desire his jewels, and this other's[51] house,
And my more-having would be as a sauce
To make me hunger more,[52] that I should forge
Quarrels unjust against the good and loyal,
Destroying them for wealth.

---

[44] 2 Peter 2:19.

[45] Indulging the sinful nature instead of heeding prudence and wisdom leads to the downfall of kings.

[46] Don't be afraid to take the crown.

[47] Macduff assures Malcolm that he could deceive everyone by satisfying his lust but appear virtuous in the light. 1 Timothy 5:24; Luke 12:2-3.

[48] There are plenty of women who would want to sleep with the king.

[49] He can't be so insatiable so as to use up every woman. Unfortunately, here Macduff is justifying a lot of means to the end of usurping Macbeth. He is certain that Malcolm can't be so far gone as to be irredeemable. But the unruled self is no leader. Galatians 5:19-21; Proverbs 25:28.

[50] Evil disposition.

[51] Another's.

[52] The more he takes, the more he wants. Proverbs 30:11-14 encompasses what Macbeth is and what Malcolm describes.

MACDUFF.

This avarice

85   Sticks deeper, grows with more pernicious root
Than summer-seeming lust, and it hath been
The sword of our slain kings.[53] Yet do not fear;
Scotland hath foisons[54] to fill up your will,
Of your mere own.[55] All these are portable,

90   With other graces weigh'd.[56]

MALCOLM.

But I have none. The king-becoming[57] graces,
As justice, verity, temp'rance, stableness,
Bounty, perseverance, mercy, lowliness,[58]
Devotion, patience, courage, fortitude,[59]

95   I have no relish of them, but abound
In the division of each several crime,[60]
Acting it many ways. Nay, had I power, I should
Pour the sweet milk of concord into hell,
Uproar the universal peace, confound

100 All unity on earth.[61]

MACDUFF.

O Scotland, Scotland!

---

[53] Greed is worse than lust for he won't outgrow it and it won't be satisfied, for in the past it has been what caused the death of kings, such as with Duncan at the hand of Macbeth.

[54] Resources.

[55] From the royal treasury, which is his by right. Certainly, his greed can be satiated with that abundance.

[56] These bad qualities are bearable when balanced with his good nature.

[57] The qualities that make a king.

[58] Humility.

[59] One might consider that what makes a good king is partly founded on what makes a good man. Proverbs 25:28; Galatians 5:22-23.

[60] For each sin he finds subdivisions to indulge.

[61] Compare with earlier scenes which described upsetting the natural order. Macbeth has already killed his kingly father, caused discord among brothers, and murdered the innocent. Malcolm is claiming he'd do the same.

MALCOLM.
   If such a one be fit to govern, speak.
   I am as I have spoken.

MACDUFF.
   Fit to govern?
   No, not to live.[62] Oh nation miserable,
   With an untitled tyrant bloody-scepter'd,[63]
105   When shalt thou see thy wholesome days again,
   Since that the truest issue of thy throne[64]
   By his own interdiction[65] stands accus'd,
   And does blaspheme his breed?[66] Thy royal father
   Was a most sainted king. The queen that bore thee,
110   Oft'ner upon her knees than on her feet,
   Died every day she lived.[67] Fare thee well!
   These evils thou repeat'st upon thyself
   Have banish'd me from Scotland.[68] Oh my breast,
   Thy hope ends here!

MALCOLM.
   Macduff, this noble passion,
115   Child of integrity,[69] hath from my soul
   Wiped the black scruples,[70] reconcil'd my thoughts

---

[62] Not only is Malcolm not fit to govern, he is not fit to live since he is so corrupted by sin. In his desperation, he tried to overcome Malcolm's vices, showing to him that he could overcome his base nature and be fit to rule. But now sees the futility of his actions.

[63] Usurping tyrant who gained the throne by murder. A beautiful summary of Macbeth's actions.

[64] The heir of the crown.

[65] Prohibiting by speech.

[66] Defames/disgraces his royal lineage.

[67] She was a woman who died to self, who was humble, who sought the will of God all her life.

[68] Because Malcolm is too evil to take back the throne, Scotland is ruined and so are Macduff's hopes of returning.

[69] Son born of uprightness.

[70] Dark misgivings/suspicions.

To thy good truth and honour.[71] Devilish Macbeth
By many of these trains hath sought to win me
Into his power,[72] and modest wisdom plucks me
120 From over-credulous haste.[73] But God above
Deal between thee and me![74] For even now
I put myself to thy direction,[75] and
Unspeak mine own detraction, here abjure
The taints and blames I laid upon myself,
125 For strangers to my nature.[76] I am yet
Unknown to woman,[77] never was forsworn,[78]
Scarcely have coveted what was mine own,[79]
At no time broke my faith,[80] would not betray
The devil to his fellow,[81] and delight
130 No less in truth than life.[82] My first false speaking
Was this upon myself.[83] What I am truly,
Is thine and my poor country's to command—[84]
Whither, indeed, before thy here-approach,[85]
Old Siward, with ten thousand warlike men,

---

[71] Now that Macduff has shown that he is a man of honor, seeking the goodness of Scotland and astonished at the self-proclaimed baseness of Malcolm despite his virtuous upbringing, Malcolm is no longer concerned about Macduff's true loyalties and so tells Macduff the truth.

[72] Macbeth has several times tried to draw him back to Scotland.

[73] But being slow to action has kept him from being gullible.

[74] "God is our witness!"

[75] "I will be guided by/put my trust in you."

[76] He takes back the former "confession," for everything he said was the exact opposite of his nature.

[77] A virgin.

[78] Does not lie.

[79] He barely wants what is belonging to him, let alone to covet another's.

[80] Never broken a promise.

[81] Would not betray the devil to himself/his kindred.

[82] He loves truth as much as life.

[83] He never lied before saying all those awful things about himself.

[84] His true nature is to serve Macduff and all of Scotland.

[85] "Before you got here."

135 Already at a point, was setting forth.[86]
Now we'll[87] together, and the chance of goodness
Be like our warranted quarrel.[88] Why are you silent?

MACDUFF.
Such welcome and unwelcome things at once[89]
'Tis hard to reconcile.

[Enter a Doctor.]

MALCOLM.
Well, more anon.[90]
140 Comes the King forth, I pray you?

DOCTOR.
Ay, sir. There are a crew of wretched souls
That stay his cure.[91] Their malady convinces[92]
The great assay of art;[93] but at his touch,
Such sanctity hath heaven given his hand,
145 They presently amend.[94]

---

[86] Siward of Northumberland is on his way with an army. This is Malcolm's uncle. Also, it should be noted that this play is semi-historical. The timing of everything is drastically shortened, as the real Malcolm was a child when his father was murdered, and several years pass before he goes to fight Macbeth.

[87] We will fight.

[88] "May the chance of success be equal to the justice of the cause."

[89] I, too, might respond this way after leaving house and home to call back this son and heir only to be told it was all for naught and then to hear his hopes uplifted. It would be quite a whirlwind. And though the end is what he hoped for, it was surely an unwelcome test. Proverbs 26:18-19.

[90] "We will speak more soon/straightaway."

[91] A group of people are waiting for him to come by and cure them. King Edward is another foil to Macbeth. He is described as saintly, full of grace and healing, as opposed to Macbeth, who is murderous and destructive.

[92] Overcomes.

[93] Efforts of modern medicine.

[94] He merely touches them, and they are healed. At this time, there developed a claim of what was called the "King's Touch" where the nobility appeared to have the gift of healing, specifically for a particular disease. It was sometimes used to determine the divine right or legitimacy of a king

MALCOLM.
I thank you, doctor.

[Exit Doctor.]

MACDUFF.
What's the disease he means?

MALCOLM.
'Tis call'd the evil.[95]
A most miraculous work in this good king,
Which often, since my here-remain[96] in England,
I have seen him do. How he solicits heaven,
150　Himself best knows; but strangely-visited[97] people,
All swoln and ulcerous, pitiful to the eye,
The mere despair of surgery,[98] he cures,
Hanging a golden stamp[99] about their necks,
Put on with holy prayers; and 'tis spoken,
155　To the succeeding royalty he leaves
The healing benediction.[100] With this strange virtue,[101]
He hath a heavenly gift of prophecy,
And sundry blessings[102] hang about his throne,
That speak him full of grace.[103]

[Enter Ross.]

---

or queen. The first to have this gift attributed to him was Edward the Confessor, who was later canonized (whether justly is up for debate).
[95] Scrofula, a form of tuberculosis. As the characters of this play are related to James I & VI, it is fitting that this ability should be brought up, not to mention that it fits the theme of a king caring for his people as his children. James I claimed to have the gift, and thus, a legitimate claim to the throne.
[96] Stay.
[97] Afflicted.
[98] Medical treatment.
[99] A coin.
[100] He passes on this gift to his children.
[101] Unique power.
[102] Many other abilities.
[103] This grace is how a king should be. Again, a sharp contrast to Macbeth.

MACDUFF.
See, who comes here?

MALCOLM.
160   My countryman, but yet I know him not.[104]

MACDUFF.
My ever-gentle[105] cousin, welcome hither.

MALCOLM.
I know him now. Good God, betimes remove
The means that makes us strangers![106]

ROSS.
Sir, amen.

MACDUFF.
Stands Scotland where it did?

ROSS.
Alas, poor country,
165   Almost afraid to know itself! It cannot
Be call'd our mother, but our grave,[107] where nothing
But who knows nothing[108] is once seen to smile;
Where sighs and groans and shrieks that rend the air
Are made, not mark'd;[109] where violent sorrow seems
170   A modern ecstasy.[110] The dead man's knell
Is there scarce ask'd for who,[111] and good men's lives
Expire before the flowers in their caps,[112]
Dying or ere they sicken.[113]

---

[104] He recognizes only his dress as someone from Scotland, not the man.
[105] Noble, as in a gentleman.
[106] "Dear God, quickly end the circumstances that separate brothers."
[107] No longer the place where they were born but the place where they die.
[108] No one except a clueless person
[109] Unnoticed. These pitiful sounds have become commonplace.
[110] A common emotion.
[111] No one asks for whom rings the funeral toll.
[112] Men die before the flowers in their caps wilt.
[113] They die before they even fall sick.

MACDUFF.

    O, relation[114]

    Too nice,[115] and yet too true!

MALCOLM.

    What's the newest grief?

ROSS.

175   That of an hour's age doth hiss the speaker;

    Each minute teems a new one.[116]

MACDUFF.

    How does my wife?

ROSS.

    Why, well.[117]

MACDUFF.

    And all my children?

ROSS.

    Well too.

MACDUFF.

    The tyrant has not batter'd at their peace?[118]

ROSS.

    No, they were well at peace when I did leave 'em.

MACDUFF.

180   Be not a niggard[119] of your speech. How goes't?

---

[114] Report.

[115] Poetic.

[116] People rebuke the person who reports old news that's only an hour hold. Every moment brings a new event.

[117] He does not elaborate and uses this word three times. And there is a double meaning in it. They were well and alive when he left them, but shortly thereafter were killed and are now at peace in the grave.

[118] He asks if Macbeth has attacked them. But for the listener, they might hear the irony of disturbing their rest in the grave.

[119] Stingy, dodging.

ROSS.

When I came hither to transport the tidings,
Which I have heavily[120] borne, there ran a rumour
Of many worthy fellows[121] that were out,[122]
Which was to my belief witness'd the rather
185   For that I saw the tyrant's power afoot. [123]
Now is the time of help. *[To Malcolm.]* Your eye in Scotland
Would create soldiers, make our women fight,
To doff[124] their dire distresses.

MALCOLM.

Be't their comfort
We are coming thither. Gracious England hath
190   Lent us good Siward and ten thousand men;
An older and a better soldier none
That Christendom gives out.

ROSS.

Would I could answer
This comfort with the like! But I have words
That would[125] be howl'd out in the desert air,
195   Where hearing should not latch them.[126]

MACDUFF.

What concern they?
The general cause? Or is it a fee-grief
Due to some single breast?[127]

ROSS.

No mind that's honest
But in it shares some woe,[128] though the main part

---

[120] Sadly.

[121] Good men.

[122] Exiled.

[123] His belief in the rumor was strengthened when he saw Macbeth's army.

[124] Put off, as opposed to "don."

[125] Should.

[126] Where no one could hear it.

[127] "Does this affect everyone or just one of us?"

[128] "No decent man could help but share in the sorrow."

Pertains to you alone.

MACDUFF.
    If it be mine,
200   Keep it not from me; quickly let me have it.

ROSS.
    Let not your ears despise my tongue forever,
    Which shall possess them[129] with the heaviest sound
    That ever yet they heard.

MACDUFF.
    Hum! I guess at it.

ROSS.
    Your castle is surpris'd,[130] your wife and babes
205   Savagely slaughter'd. To relate the manner
    Were, on the quarry of these murder'd deer,[131]
    To add the death of you.[132]

MALCOLM.
    Merciful heaven!
    What, man, ne'er pull your hat upon your brows.[133]
    Give sorrow words. The grief that does not speak
210   Whispers the o'er-fraught heart, and bids it break.[134]

MACDUFF.
    My children too?

ROSS.
    Wife, children, servants, all
    That could be found.

---

[129] Make Macduff's ears possess Ross' tongue's words
[130] Ambushed.
[131] A quarry is the heap of animals after a hunt, playing on the words "deer" and "dear."
[132] "To tell you how they were killed would kill you too."
[133] "Don't hide your grief."
[134] There is little to say other than this passage touches the heart. How true it is that a hidden grief will eat away at the soul.

135

MACDUFF.
And I must be from thence!
My wife kill'd too?

ROSS.
I have said.

MALCOLM.
Be comforted.
Let's make us med'cines of our great revenge
215   To cure this deadly grief.

MACDUFF.
He has no children.[135] All my pretty ones?
Did you say all? Oh hell-kite![136] All?
What, all my pretty chickens and their dam[137]
At one fell swoop?

MALCOLM.
220   Dispute it like a man.

MACDUFF.
I shall do so,
But I must also feel it as a man.[138]
I cannot but remember such things were,
That were most precious to me. Did heaven look on,
And would not take their part?[139] Sinful Macduff,
225   They were all struck for thee! Naught that I am,
Not for their own demerits, but for mine,
Fell slaughter on their souls. Heaven rest them now!

---

[135] Of himself or Macbeth.
[136] A kite is a bird of prey. Here, Macduff insults Macbeth by calling him
a bird from hell, a hellishly cruel person.
[137] Innocent, defenseless birds.
[138] Again, what are the things that make a man? He will take revenge on
the murder of his wife and children, and he will mourn them as a man who
deeply loves those that were his.
[139] An honest response from a grieving heart.

MALCOLM.

Be this the whetstone of your sword. Let grief
Convert to anger; blunt not the heart, enrage it.

MACDUFF.

230   Oh, I could play the woman with mine eyes
And braggart with my tongue![140] But, gentle heavens,
Cut short all intermission.[141] Front to front
Bring thou this fiend of Scotland and myself;[142]
Within my sword's length set him. If he 'scape,
235   Heaven forgive him too![143]

MALCOLM.

This tune goes manly.
Come, go we to the King.[144] Our power is ready;
Our lack is nothing but our leave.[145] Macbeth
Is ripe for shaking, and the powers above
Put on their instruments.[146] Receive what cheer you may.
240   The night is long that never finds the day.[147]

[Exeunt.]

---

[140] "I could be womanly and weep and make boasts on my revenge."

[141] "Heaven, don't make me wait."

[142] "Bring Macbeth and I face to face."

[143] A thing Macduff does not want to happen, so he will not let him escape.

[144] Edward of England.

[145] The army is ready. All they lack now is to say goodbye and move.

[146] Malcolm says they are heaven's instruments of justice.

[147] Another clever piece of insight from Malcolm. He pushed Macduff to morn, and then to take up the manly shield. Now he tells them to be of good cheer. He is a good kingly figure. A new day is coming, and especially for those who look on in hope.

ACT V[1]

SCENE I. Dunsinane. A room in the castle.

Enter a Doctor of Physic and a Waiting-Gentlewoman.

DOCTOR.
I have two nights watched with you, but can perceive no truth in your report. When was it she last walked?

GENTLEWOMAN.
Since his Majesty went into the field,[2] I have seen her rise from her bed, throw her nightgown upon her, unlock her closet, take
5   forth paper, fold it, write upon't, read it, afterwards seal it, and again return to bed; yet all this while in a most fast sleep.

DOCTOR.
A great perturbation[3] in nature,[4] to receive at once the benefit of sleep, and do the effects of watching.[5] In this slumbery agitation, besides her walking and other actual performances, what, at any
10   time, have you heard her say?

GENTLEWOMAN.
That, sir, which I will not report after her.[6]

DOCTOR.
You may to me, and 'tis most meet[7] you should.

GENTLEWOMAN.
Neither to you nor anyone, having no witness to confirm my speech.

---

[1] This last act appears to be happening almost simultaneously, or at least the scenes are partly overlapping. Imagine a film where the screen cuts back and forth quickly, heightening the intensity of the action as the story ends.
[2] Macbeth is at war.
[3] Mental confusion.
[4] What is happening in her mind is unnatural.
[5] Acts as though she is awake.
[6] "I will not repeat what she says."
[7] Suitable, proper.

[Enter Lady Macbeth with a taper.[8]]

15   Lo you, here she comes! This is her very guise, and, upon my life, fast asleep. Observe her. Stand close.[9]

DOCTOR.
How came she by that light?

GENTLEWOMAN.
Why, it stood by her. She has light by her continually.[10] 'Tis her command.

DOCTOR.
20   You see, her eyes are open.

GENTLEWOMAN.
Ay, but their sense are shut.

DOCTOR.
What is it she does now? Look how she rubs her hands.

GENTLEWOMAN.
It is an accustomed action with her, to seem thus washing her hands. I have known her continue in this a quarter of an hour.

LADY MACBETH.
25   Yet here's a spot.

DOCTOR.
Hark, she speaks. I will set down[11] what comes from her, to satisfy[12] my remembrance the more strongly.

---

[8] A candle.

[9] This whole scene is most fascinating. While Lady Macbeth is the central figure, it is almost as if she is a ghost among the living. She is a shell of the person she was before she first read that letter. But since then, she can do nothing but repeat the night Duncan was murdered.

[10] They thought themselves friend of the darkness, that it might hide their deeds. But the darkness abandoned them to fear, and the light brings little comfort now.

[11] Write down.

[12] Support.

LADY MACBETH.

Out, damned spot! Out, I say! One, two. Why, then 'tis time to do't. Hell is murky.[13] Fie,[14] my lord, fie! A soldier, and afeard?[15]
30   What need we fear who knows it, when none can call our power to account? Yet who would have thought the old man to have had so much blood in him?[16]

DOCTOR.

Do you mark that?

LADY MACBETH.

The Thane of Fife had a wife. Where is she now?[17]—What, will
35   these hands ne'er be clean?—No more o'that, my lord, no more o'that; you mar all with this starting.[18]

DOCTOR.

Go to, go to.[19] You have known what you should not.

GENTLEWOMAN.

She has spoke what she should not, I am sure of that. Heaven knows what she has known.[20]

LADY MACBETH.

40   Here's the smell of the blood still. All the perfumes of Arabia will not sweeten this little hand. Oh, oh, oh!

DOCTOR.

What a sigh is there! The heart is sorely charged.[21]

---

[13] A particularly disturbing line. Not only were their actions murky morally, but now she sits in deep, confusing, fearful, solitary, condemning darkness with no way out. She has created a hell for herself.

[14] An exclamation or interjection of disapproval. "Improper."

[15] She is transported back to that night when she called Macbeth unmanly.

[16] The blood bears witness and marks their souls and minds. Genesis 4:10, 9:6; Proverbs 1:16-19, 28:17.

[17] Referring to Macduff's wife.

[18] "You'll ruin everything by being constantly startled."

[19] A statement of disbelief or disapproval. "For shame!"

[20] A double meaning. "Heaven knows" is both a statement of "nobody knows" and "God knows what you have done."

[21] Heavy, weighed down.

GENTLEWOMAN.
I would not have such a heart in my bosom for the dignity of the whole body.[22]

DOCTOR.
45   Well, well, well.[23]

GENTLEWOMAN.
Pray God it be, sir.[24]

DOCTOR.
This disease is beyond my practice. Yet I have known those which have walked in their sleep who have died holily in their beds.[25]

LADY MACBETH.
50   Wash your hands, put on your nightgown; look not so pale! I tell you yet again, Banquo's buried. He cannot come out on's grave.[26]

DOCTOR.
Even so?

LADY MACBETH.
To bed, to bed. There's knocking at the gate.[27] Come, come,
55   come, come, give me your hand. What's done cannot be undone. To bed, to bed, to bed.

[Exit Lady Macbeth.]

DOCTOR.
Will she go now to bed?

---

[22] "I wouldn't take that heart even if I was made queen." Dramatic irony, as the listener knows that is exactly what Lady Macbeth traded.
[23] "Dear me."
[24] Playing on the doctor's statement, "Pray it turns out well!"
[25] People can walk in their sleep and still be innocent.
[26] All three murders have been accounted for here.
[27] Consider the knocking at the gate with the porter pretending to be Hell's gatekeeper in 2.3.

GENTLEWOMAN.
Directly.

DOCTOR.
Foul whisp'rings[28] are abroad. Unnatural deeds
60   Do breed unnatural troubles.[29] Infected minds
To their deaf pillows will discharge their secrets.[30]
More needs she the divine than the physician.[31]
God, God, forgive us all! Look after her;
Remove from her the means of all annoyance,[32]
65   And still keep eyes upon her.[33] So, good night.
My mind she has mated,[34] and amaz'd my sight.
I think, but dare not speak.

GENTLEWOMAN.
Good night, good doctor.

[Exeunt.]

---

[28] Evil rumors. He has probably heard suggestion of the Macbeths' guilt.
[29] Consider the note on the furies in 3.4. Further, unnatural can also mean supernatural, so her immoral deeds have reaped spiritual consequences.
[30] The guilty will confess their deeds while they sleep.
[31] How true this is! Sadly, she has rejected such help.
[32] Means of harming herself.
[33] Watch her constantly.
[34] Overcome, put in checkmate.

SCENE II. The country near Dunsinane.

Drum and colours. Enter Menteith, Caithness, Angus, Lennox, and Soldiers.

MENTEITH.

The English power[1] is near, led on by Malcolm,
His uncle Siward, and the good Macduff.
Revenges burn in them, for their dear causes
Would to the bleeding and the grim alarm

5   Excite the mortified man.[2]

ANGUS.

Near Birnam wood
Shall we well meet them; that way are they coming.

CAITHNESS.

Who knows if Donalbain be with his brother?

LENNOX.

For certain, sir, he is not. I have a file[3]
Of all the gentry. There is Siward's son

10   And many unrough[4] youths, that even now
Protest their first of manhood.[5]

MENTEITH.

What does the tyrant?

CAITHNESS.

Great Dunsinane he strongly fortifies.
Some say he's mad,[6] others that lesser hate him[7]
Do call it valiant fury;[8] but, for certain,

---

[1] Army.

[2] Their right anger and violent call to battle would waken even the dead to their cause.

[3] Roster.

[4] Beardless, untried, young.

[5] This battle will make men of them.

[6] He's gone insane.

[7] What a backhanded statement!

[8] Brave anger, excused by the war, perhaps.

143

15   He cannot buckle[9] his distemper'd[10] cause
      Within the belt of rule.[11]

ANGUS.
    Now does he feel
    His secret murders sticking on his hands;[12]
    Now minutely revolts upbraid his faith-breach.[13]
    Those he commands move only in command,
20   Nothing in love.[14] Now does he feel his title
    Hang loose about him, like a giant's robe
    Upon a dwarfish thief.[15]

MENTEITH.
    Who, then, shall blame
    His pester'd[16] senses to recoil and start,
    When all that is within him does condemn
25   Itself for being there?[17]

CAITHNESS.
    Well, march we on,
    To give obedience where 'tis truly ow'd.
    Meet we the med'cine of the sickly weal,[18]
    And with him pour we in our country's purge
    Each drop of us.[19]

---

[9] Restrain, control.

[10] Disturbed, ill, unnatural.

[11] He is uncontrolled, another mark of unmanliness.

[12] Reflective of Lady Macbeth.

[13] Regular revolts punish him for violating his vows to Duncan, his people, and God.

[14] They follow orders, but neither respect Macbeth nor believe in the cause.

[15] The mantle of king is meant for a great man.

[16] Troubled.

[17] His conscience condemns him, so it is understandable that he's gone mad.

[18] "We meet with him (Malcolm) who will heal our nation." A weal is a raised spot on one's skin.

[19] "Together we pour out our blood to cleanse the land."

LENNOX.
    Or so much as it needs[20]

30   To dew the sovereign flower and drown the weeds.
    Make we our march towards Birnam.[21]

[Exeunt, marching.]

---

[20] Playing off of "purge," this was probably referencing bloodletting, so he says to only give as much blood as needed, which in the following statement is "to water the new king and drown his enemies that are choking out goodness."

[21] The first part of the prophecy the three weird sisters gave to Macbeth in 4.1 is coming to pass.

SCENE III. Dunsinane. A room in the castle.

Enter Macbeth, Doctor, and Attendants.

MACBETH.

Bring me no more reports; let them fly all.[1]

Till Birnam wood remove to Dunsinane

I cannot taint[2] with fear.[3] What's the boy Malcolm?

Was he not born of woman? The spirits that know

5   All mortal consequences[4] have pronounc'd me thus:

"Fear not, Macbeth. No man that's born of woman

Shall e'er have power upon thee." Then fly, false thanes,

And mingle with the English epicures![5]

The mind I sway[6] by and the heart I bear

10   Shall never sag with doubt nor shake with fear.

[Enter a Servant.]

The devil damn thee black, thou cream-fac'd loon![7]

Where gott'st thou that goose[8] look?

SERVANT.

There is ten thousand—

MACBETH.

Geese,[9] villain?[10]

SERVANT.

Soldiers, sir.

---

[1] "Them" being the thanes who have deserted. He no longer wants to hear of another thane who has abandoned him.

[2] Infect, become overwhelmed by.

[3] And why should he care? He needn't be afraid until Birnam Forest moves, which it cannot do.

[4] "Spirits that know everything that happens with mortals."

[5] As in epicurean, the English gluttons, or pleasure-seekers.

[6] Guides himself.

[7] The servant is white with fear. Also, a loon would be a stupid person.

[8] A simpleton. Here, birds are used as insults, representing negative characteristics in a person.

[9] Foolish people, but also returning to him calling the servant a goose.

[10] Commoner, nobody.

MACBETH.
  Go prick thy face and over-red thy fear,[11]
15   Thou lily-liver'd[12] boy. What soldiers, patch?[13]
  Death of thy soul![14] Those linen cheeks of thine
  Are counsellors to fear.[15] What soldiers, whey-face?[16]

SERVANT.
  The English force, so please you.

MACBETH.
  Take thy face hence.[17]

                    [Exit Servant.]

  Seyton![18]—I am sick at heart,
20   When I behold[19]—Seyton, I say!—This push[20]
  Will cheer[21] me ever or disseat[22] me now.
  I have liv'd long enough. My way of life
  Is fall'n into the sere,[23] the yellow leaf,
  And that which should accompany old age,
25   As honour, love, obedience, troops of friends,

---

[11] "Get some color in your pale/fearful face."

[12] A liver without blood is a dead one.

[13] Fool.

[14] An oath, and a rather vile one, to hope someone's soul dies eternally.

[15] Having the servant go about white-faced will encourage others to become afraid.

[16] Macbeth is unable to go a sentence without insulting his servant. He is a shell of the man he once was, and clearly afraid and insane.

[17] My favorite insult of Macbeth's.

[18] A sexton is an officer or custodian of a church. He might deal with religious objects or even attend to graves. But what is a Seyton? There is no such position, so Macbeth calls for a servant named "Seyton." Likely, we are to read this as "Satan." It is unlikely an accident that Macbeth calls for him three times.

[19] Behold what? A fearful man? Himself? Another vision?

[20] Effort, battle.

[21] "Chair," secure.

[22] Overthrow.

[23] Withered, barren.

I must not look to have,[24] but, in their stead,
Curses, not loud but deep,[25] mouth-honour,[26] breath
Which the poor heart would fain deny, and dare not.[27]
Seyton!—

[Enter Seyton.]

SEYTON.
30   What's your gracious pleasure?

MACBETH.
       What news more?

SEYTON.
       All is confirm'd, my lord, which was reported.

MACBETH.
       I'll fight till from my bones my flesh be hack'd.
       Give me my armour.

SEYTON.
       'Tis not needed yet.

MACBETH.
       I'll put it on.
35   Send out more horses, skirr[28] the country round.
       Hang those that talk of fear. Give me mine armour.
       How does your patient, Doctor?

DOCTOR.
       Not so sick, my lord,
       As she is troubled with thick-coming fancies,[29]
       That keep her from her rest.

---

[24] All the good things a long, upright life should have brought he will not
have. Instead, he has had a short, troubled life that ends in disrepute, hate,
and rebellion. Also, consider Sonnet 73 and contrast it to this speech.
[25] Deadly whispered curses.
[26] Essentially double-tongued.
[27] "My heart would gladly end my life, but I dare not do it."
[28] Scour, skirt.
[29] Endless visions.

MACBETH.
Cure her of that.
40 Canst thou not minister to a mind diseas'd,
Pluck from the memory a rooted sorrow,
Raze out the written troubles of the brain,
And with some sweet oblivious antidote
Cleanse the stuff'd bosom of that perilous stuff
45 Which weighs upon the heart?[30]

DOCTOR.
Therein the patient
Must minister to himself.

MACBETH.
Throw physic[31] to the dogs! I'll none of it.
Come, put mine armour on. Give me my staff.
Seyton, send out.[32] Doctor, the Thanes fly from me.—
50 Come, sir, dispatch.[33]—If thou couldst, Doctor, cast
The water[34] of my land[35], find her disease,
And purge it to a sound and pristine health,
I would applaud thee to the very echo[36]
That should applaud again.—Pull't off, I say.—
55 What rhubarb, senna,[37] or what purgative drug,
Would scour[38] these English hence? Hear'st thou of them?

---

[30] While the doctor says the patient must do this herself, truly this is a spiritual matter. Lady Macbeth's cure is in repentance, her soul needs to be ministered by forgiveness from the One who forgets our wrongdoing when it was erased and cleansed by Blood. Macbeth wishes that her wrongdoing might be cured by medicine or a concoction that will dull her into forgetfulness. But this will not cleanse her, only dull the pain for a time.
[31] Medicine.
[32] Send out soldiers.
[33] Hurry.
[34] Urine (to discover a sickness).
[35] Scotland.
[36] Applaud so much the sound will echo.
[37] Both plants used in medicine to cleanse.
[38] Purge, rid.

DOCTOR.
 Ay, my good lord. Your royal preparation
 Makes us hear something.[39]

MACBETH.
 Bring it after me.—
 I will not be afraid of death and bane[40]
60 Till Birnam forest come to Dunsinane.

[Exeunt all except Doctor.]

DOCTOR.
 Were I from Dunsinane away and clear,
 Profit again should hardly draw me here.[41]

[Exit.]

---

[39] "You're preparing for war makes us hear something." But the vagueness
of this statement shows his lack of commitment.
[40] Ruin.
[41] "If I was as far from Dunsinane as I could be, I couldn't be paid to come
back."

SCENE IV. The country near Birnam Wood.

Drum and colours.[1] Enter Malcolm, Siward, Macduff, Siward's son, Menteith, Caithness, Angus, and Soldiers, marching.

MALCOLM.
　　Cousins, I hope the days are near at hand
　　That chambers will be safe.[2]

MENTEITH.
　　We doubt it nothing.

SIWARD.
　　What wood is this before us?

MENTEITH.
　　The wood of Birnam.

MALCOLM.
　　Let every soldier hew him down a bough,
5　　And bear't before him. Thereby shall we shadow[3]
　　The numbers of our host, and make discovery[4]
　　Err in report of us.

SOLDIERS.
　　It shall be done.

SIWARD.
　　We learn no other but[5] the confident tyrant
　　Keeps[6] still in Dunsinane, and will endure[7]
10　　Our setting down before't.[8]

MALCOLM.
　　'Tis his main hope;

---

[1] The flags and standards with the coat of arms of each man's house.
[2] People will be safe in their bedrooms/homes.
[3] Conceal, disguise.
[4] Scouts.
[5] Have no news except
[6] Remains.
[7] Not prevent.
[8] Laying siege to the castle.

152

For where there is advantage to be given,
Both more and less have given him the revolt,
And none serve with him but constrainèd things
Whose hearts are absent too.[9]

MACDUFF.
Let our just censures
15   Attend the true event,[10] and put we on
Industrious soldiership.

SIWARD.
The time approaches
That will with due decision make us know
What we shall say we have and what we owe.[11]
Thoughts speculative their unsure hopes relate,[12]
20   But certain issue strokes must arbitrate—[13]
Towards which advance the war.[14]

[Exeunt, marching.]

---

[9] Macbeth wants them to lay siege to the castle because that is his only advantage due to his men deserting. The only ones left fight because they have been forced, not because they want to. He is absent of men and their loyalty.
[10] "Let us refrain from judgement/certainty until events have happened."
[11] "The time soon will tell with certainty what we do or do not have."
[12] "Sitting around theorizing won't make anything reality."
[13] "We will only settle matters by fighting."
[14] "With that goal, let us begin."

SCENE V. Dunsinane. Within the castle.

Enter Macbeth, Seyton, and Soldiers, with drum and colours.

MACBETH.

    Hang out our banners on the outward walls.

    The cry is still, "They come!" Our castle's strength

    Will laugh a siege to scorn. Here let them lie

    Till famine and the ague[1] eat them up.

5   Were they not forc'd with those that should be ours,[2]

    We might have met them dareful, beard to beard,[3]

    And beat them backward home.

[A cry of women within.]

    What is that noise?

SEYTON.

    It is the cry of women, my good lord.

MACBETH.

    I have almost forgot the taste of fears.

10   The time has been, my senses would have cool'd[4]

    To hear a night-shriek,[5] and my fell[6] of hair

    Would at a dismal treatise rouse and stir[7]

    As life were in't. I have supp'd full with horrors;[8]

    Direness, familiar to my slaughterous thoughts,

15   Cannot once start me. Wherefore was that cry?

SEYTON.

    The Queen, my lord, is dead.

---

[1] Fever.

[2] Reinforced with men that should have defended Macbeth.

[3] Boldly, man to man.

[4] Chilled by fear.

[5] Consider 2.2.

[6] Skin, as in a hide of an animal. Related to "pelt."

[7] "Would at a sad account/tale stand on end"

[8] "I have had had my fill of horrors."

MACBETH.

She should have died hereafter;[9]
There would have been a time for such a word.

Tomorrow, and tomorrow, and tomorrow,
20   Creeps in this petty pace from day to day,[10]
To the last syllable of recorded time,
And all our yesterdays have lighted fools[11]
The way to dusty death.[12] Out, out, brief candle![13]
Life's but a walking shadow,[14] a poor player
25   That struts and frets his hour upon the stage
And then is heard no more.[15] It is a tale
Told by an idiot, full of sound and fury,
Signifying nothing.[16]

[Enter a Messenger.]

Thou com'st to use thy tongue; thy story quickly.

---

[9] She would have died anyway/after the battle/at a more appropriate time. His love for her is gone. She is an annoyance now. His corruption has consumed all of his love and whatever bit of good was left in him.

[10] Proverbs 27:1.

[11] Every day we travel takes us one day closer to our death, and as a candle walks us to our beds, so the sun (or perhaps the Word?) lighted the path we walked until we sleep. For him, the light deceives. Or perhaps it is the forerunner to the next statement, and this light only creates our shadowed life.

[12] Genesis 3:19; Job 34:15; Psalm 90:3, 9; Ecclesiastes 3:20, 12:7.

[13] James 4:14.

[14] Job 8:9, 14:1-2.

[15] "Like an actor that worries about his brief time on stage and then no one remembers him is the man who worries about his life to be no more." James 4:14; Matthew 6:25.

[16] This is another of Shakespeare's most famous soliloquies, and part of this speech is used as a title of a book by Faulkner. It is also a most depressing look on life. To think we are nothing more than actors, that our life is to do what we can for ourselves and then turn to nothing but dust, that our lives and beliefs are meaningless, would bring a deep despair. But it is also an understandable perspective from Macbeth at this moment. He has lost friends, respect, and now his wife to madness and suicide. This is a nihilistic look on the futility of life, one that can come only from someone who has lost all meaning, hope, and light from his life.

MESSENGER.

30   Gracious my lord,
        I should report that which I say I saw,
        But know not how to do't.

MACBETH.
        Well, say, sir.

MESSENGER.
        As I did stand my watch upon the hill,
        I look'd toward Birnam, and anon[17], methought,
35   The wood began to move.

MACBETH.
        Liar and slave!

MESSENGER.
        Let me endure your wrath if't be not so.
        Within this three mile may you see it coming.
        I say, a moving grove.

MACBETH.
        If thou speak'st false,
        Upon the next tree shalt thou hang alive
40   Till famine cling[18] thee. If thy speech be sooth[19],
        I care not if thou dost for me as much.[20]
        I pull in resolution,[21] and begin
        To doubt th' equivocation[22] of the fiend[23]
        That lies like truth. "Fear not, till Birnam wood
45   Do come to Dunsinane," and now a wood
        Comes toward Dunsinane.[24] Arm, arm, and out!

---

[17] At once.

[18] Shrivel.

[19] Truth.

[20] If what he says is true, he can hang Macbeth on a tree.

[21] Take back his confidence.

[22] Ambiguous voice, double tongue. Also, consider 2.3.

[23] Adversary, the Devil.

[24] Technically, they didn't lie. They merely gave him false confidence.

If this which he avouches[25] does appear,
There is nor flying hence nor tarrying here.[26]
I 'gin to be aweary of the sun,
50   And wish th'estate o'th'world were now undone.[27]
Ring the alarum bell! Blow, wind, come wrack,[28]
At least we'll die with harness[29] on our back.

[Exeunt.]

---

[25] If what the messenger claims.

[26] No use running or standing here.

[27] He grows weary of life and would like to see the order of the world (nature) turned to chaos.

[28] Ruin.

[29] Armor.

SCENE VI. The same. A plain before the castle.

Drum and colours. Enter Malcolm, Siward, Macduff, and their Army, with boughs.

MALCOLM.
Now near enough.[1] Your leafy screens throw down,
And show like those[2] you are. You, worthy uncle,
Shall with my cousin, your right noble son,
Lead our first battle. Worthy Macduff and we
5   Shall take upon's what else remains to do,
According to our order.[3]

SIWARD.
Fare you well.
Do[4] we but find the tyrant's power[5] tonight,
Let us be beaten if we cannot fight.

MACDUFF.
Make all our trumpets speak! Give them all breath,
10   Those clamorous harbingers[6] of blood and death.

[Exeunt. Alarums continued.]

---

[1] "We are close enough."
[2] And appear as what.
[3] The battle plan.
[4] If.
[5] Army.
[6] Forerunners.

SCENE VII. The same. Another part of the plain.

Enter Macbeth.

MACBETH.
They have tied me to a stake. I cannot fly,[1]
But, bear-like I must fight the course.[2] What's[3] he
That was not born of woman? Such a one
Am I to fear, or none.

[Enter young Siward.]

YOUNG SIWARD.
5   What is thy name?

MACBETH.
Thou'lt be afraid to hear it.

YOUNG SIWARD.
No, though thou call'st thyself a hotter name
Than any is in hell.

MACBETH.
My name's Macbeth.

YOUNG SIWARD.
The devil himself could not pronounce a title
More hateful to mine ear.

MACBETH.
No, nor more fearful.

YOUNG SIWARD.
10   Thou liest, abhorrèd tyrant. With my sword
I'll prove the lie thou speak'st.

[They fight, and young Siward is slain.]

---

[1] Reminiscent of Banquo's and Macduff's families and their last words.
[2] A round of bearbaiting was called a course. So, Macbeth, like a bear, has been tied to a stake and the dogs surround him.
[3] Who is.

MACBETH.

    Thou wast born of woman.

    But swords I smile at, weapons laugh to scorn,

    Brandish'd by man that's of a woman born.

[Exit.]⁴

[Alarums. Enter Macduff.]

MACDUFF.

15   That way the noise is. Tyrant, show thy face!

    If thou be'st slain and with no stroke of mine,

    My wife and children's ghosts will haunt me still.

    I cannot strike at wretched kerns,⁵ whose arms

    Are hired to bear their staves.⁶ Either thou, Macbeth,

20   Or else my sword with an unbatter'd edge

    I sheathe again undeeded.⁷ There thou shouldst be;

    By this great clatter, one of greatest note

    Seems bruited.⁸ ⁹ Let me find him, Fortune,

    And more I beg not.

[Exit. Alarums.]

[Enter Malcolm and Siward.]

SIWARD.

25   This way, my lord. The castle's gently render'd.¹⁰

    The tyrant's people on both sides do fight,

    The noble thanes do bravely in the war,

    The day almost itself professes yours,

    And little is to do.

---

⁴ Presumably, Macbeth takes Siward's son's body with him. Rather like he is dragging him to hell if you consider it.

⁵ Foot soldiers.

⁶ The Irish were paid to fight, just like Macdonwald.

⁷ "Either I sheathe my sword in you, or it returns to its scabbard unused."

⁸ Reported, rumored.

⁹ "You must be over there. This noise sounds like one of rank is being announced."

¹⁰ Easily surrendered.

MALCOLM.
　　We have met with foes
30　　That strike beside us.[11]

SIWARD.
　　Enter, sir, the castle.

　　　　　　　　　　[Exeunt. Alarum.]

---

[11] Fight for them/miss them on purpose.

SCENE VIII. The same. Another part of the field.[1]

Enter Macbeth.

MACBETH.

    Why should I play the Roman fool and die
    On mine own sword?[2] Whiles I see lives, the gashes
    Do better upon them.[3]

[Enter Macduff.]

MACDUFF.

    Turn, hell-hound, turn!

MACBETH.

    Of all men else I have avoided thee.

5   But get thee back! My soul is too much charg'd[4]
    With blood of thine already.

MACDUFF.

    I have no words;
    My voice is in my sword, thou bloodier villain
    Than terms can give thee out!

[They fight. Alarum.]

MACBETH.

    Thou losest labour.[5]
    As easy mayst thou the intrenchant[6] air

10   With thy keen sword impress[7] as make me bleed.
    Let fall thy blade on vulnerable crests;
    I bear a charmèd life which must not yield
    To one of woman born.

---

[1] The First Folio has this scene as a continuation of the previous.
[2] Suicide like historic Romans such as Brutus or Marc Antony.
[3] "As long as I see enemies, my cuts would be better for them."
[4] Burdened, guilty.
[5] "You're wasting effort."
[6] Not able to be cut.
[7] "You might as well try to cut the air."

MACDUFF.

Despair thy charm,
And let the angel[8] whom thou still hast serv'd
15   Tell thee, Macduff was from his mother's womb
Untimely ripp'd.[9]

MACBETH.

Accursèd be that tongue that tells me so,
For it hath cow'd my better part of man![10]
And be these juggling[11] fiends no more believ'd
20   That palter with us in a double sense,[12]
That keep the word of promise to our ear
And break it to our hope.[13] I'll not fight with thee.

MACDUFF.

Then yield thee, coward,
And live to be the show and gaze[14] o'th'time.
25   We'll have thee, as our rarer monsters are,
Painted upon a pole,[15] and underwrit,
"Here may you see the tyrant."

MACBETH.

I will not yield
To kiss the ground before young Malcolm's feet,
And to be baited with the rabble's curse.[16]
30   Though Birnam wood be come to Dunsinane,
And thou oppos'd, being of no woman born,

---

[8] Evil spirit.

[9] Prematurely cut out, a cesarean delivery. Remember the apparition of the bloody baby from 4.1.

[10] Frightened his courage.

[11] Deceiving.

[12] Equivocate, speak with a double tongue.

[13] "They make promises we think we understand and then crush our hopes when their deception is revealed."

[14] Spectacle.

[15] Painted on a sign (like an advertisement of the most curious object to see) or perhaps hung in cage (or by the neck).

[16] Taunted by commoners.

Yet I will try the last. Before my body
I throw my warlike shield. Lay on,[17] Macduff,
And damn'd be him that first cries, "Hold, enough!"[18]

[Exeunt fighting. Alarums.]
[They enter fighting, and Macbeth is slain.]
[Exit Macduff with Macbeth's body.]

[Retreat and flourish. Enter, with drum and colours, Malcolm, Siward, Ross, Thanes and Soldiers.]

MALCOLM.
35   I would the friends we miss were safe arriv'd.[19]

SIWARD.
Some must go off; and yet, by these I see
So great a day as this is cheaply bought.[20]

MALCOLM.
Macduff is missing, and your noble son.

ROSS.
Your son, my lord, has paid a soldier's debt.
40   He only liv'd but till he was a man,
The which no sooner had his prowess confirm'd[21]
In the unshrinking station where he fought,
But like a man he died.[22]

SIWARD.
Then he is dead?

ROSS.
Ay, and brought off the field. Your cause of sorrow
45   Must not be measur'd by his worth, for then
It hath no end.

---

[17] "Come at me."
[18] "Damned be the first person that yields."
[19] "I wish all of our friends had survived."
[20] "All war costs lives, yet this one cost us surprisingly little."
[21] "He lived long enough to prove he was a man."
[22] A man is one who fights with honor.

SIWARD.
Had he his hurts before?[23]

ROSS.
Ay, on the front.

SIWARD.
Why then, God's soldier be he!
Had I as many sons as I have hairs,
I would not wish them to a fairer death.
50   And so his knell is knoll'd.[24]

MALCOLM.
He's worth more sorrow,
And that I'll spend for him.

SIWARD.
He's worth no more.
They say he parted well and paid his score,
And so, God be with him! Here comes newer comfort.

[Enter Macduff with Macbeth's head.]

MACDUFF.
Hail, King, for so thou art. Behold, where stands[25]
55   Th' usurper's cursèd head. The time is free.
I see thee compass'd with thy kingdom's pearl[26]
That speak my salutation in their minds,
Whose voices I desire aloud with mine:
Hail, King of Scotland!

ALL.
Hail, King of Scotland!

[Flourish.]

---

[23] "Were his wounds on the front of him?" Basically, did he die fleeing or did he face death like a man of courage?
[24] "His funeral song has played and ended."
[25] On a pole.
[26] Encircled with nobles as a crown with jewels.

165

MALCOLM.
60   We shall not spend a large expense of time
       Before we reckon with your several loves
       And make us even with you.[27] My thanes and kinsmen,
       Henceforth be earls, the first that ever Scotland
       In such an honour nam'd. What's more to do,
65   Which would be planted newly with the time,
       As calling home our exil'd friends abroad
       That fled the snares of watchful tyranny,
       Producing forth the cruel ministers
       Of this dead butcher and his fiend-like queen—
70   Who, as 'tis thought, by self and violent hands
       Took off her life—this, and what needful else
       That calls upon us, by the grace of Grace
       We will perform in measure, time, and place.[28]
       So, thanks to all at once and to each one
75   Whom we invite to see us crown'd at Scone.

[Flourish. Exeunt Omnes.]

---

[27] "I won't dally in rewarding you all."
[28] He will restore order.

Commentary on the Birds in *Macbeth*

Macbeth is a tale of witches, deception, secrecy, and superstition. It is also a tale of loyalty, honor, relationships, and God. In reading *Macbeth,* I found myself struggling to focus on only one aspect of the play. The scriptural references and implications are numerous but typically require minimal explanation. Then there were embedded themes of fathers and children, without which much of the play would lose its depth. The consequences of rebellion and patricide cannot be overlooked, and Shakespeare does well to show the ancient theme of infuriating madness in his play. The historical connections and elaborations are fascinating to anyone, and I could not help but expound on the etymologies of some names in my notes. Further, reading this play as a married woman and young mother allowed me new insights into *Macbeth* that I failed to see in high school and college. I noticed the subtle details in the relationship between Macbeth and his wife, from fond and loving to resentful and dismissive. I felt more keenly the tenderness between Lady Macduff and her children and the pain of Macduff in his loss. But many of the central motifs of *Macbeth* revolve around nature, the supernatural, and forces untouchable. Some of these superstitions are hidden in the feathers of birds flitting throughout the play. Spurgeon, commenting on the animal imagery in Shakespeare's works, wrote, "Of the large animal group, the outstanding point is the great number drawn from birds."[1] Despite their number, they can remain unnoticed in the greater scope of his plays. I have always loved birds, and while so many themes stood out to me in this play, and I commented on them when the occasion arose in my notes, the birds stole my heart in the end. The birds in Shakespeare's *Macbeth* have a surprisingly important role in the nature of the play.

They are not placed as a background prop nor mentioned by happenstance, rather, the birds are often used to characterize a person or give added meaning to a scene's atmosphere.

Shakespeare uses the imagery of birds well, for their inclusion is both poetically beautiful and culturally significant. Even so, some of these birds are terrible omens, their presence indicating the worst of calamities. Others are a sign of prosperity and peace. Yet to the modern reader, most of these birds infer little meaning besides name, shape, and perhaps color if the reader is well-versed in bird species. Thus, explaining the symbols and omens behind the birds that Shakespeare uses is important to understanding one of the underlying messages of the play.

But before I get to the birds themselves, I want to mention some references to them. Several times, Shakespeare's characters "fly" to escape danger or are told to "take flight." The first occurrence is at the time of Banquo's murder when he tells his son, "Fly, good Fleance, fly, fly, fly!" (3.3.19). The next event is when Lennox tells another lord that some messenger needs to "fly" to England to quickly report the evils befalling the land (3.6.45-49). After her husband's flight, Lady Macduff questions Ross as to why her husband had to "fly the land," an action she calls madness (4.2.1, 3). Macbeth, frustrated with reports of the Lords who have abandoned him, brashly says, "let them fly all" (5.3.1). The last use of the word is when Macbeth relates to a snared bird, "They have tied me to a stake. I cannot fly" (5.7.1). Flight is also used in reference to Banquo's "soul's flight" to its heavenly resting place (3.1.140-141). There is also a reference to a bat's flight to the witch Hecate in order to fulfill its evil duty (3.2.40-41). While a wing is used in the witches' potion, Duncan uses the beautiful word wing to say how repayment for good deeds is slow compared to how quickly Macbeth does them (4.1.17; 1.4.16-19). Yet the crow "wings" to its home in the "rooky wood," leaving the night and evil tidings to the owl (3.2.50-51). The word "bird" is mentioned several times, but it is most touchingly used to describe Macduff's family. They are likened to the little wren, the chief bird in this book. Lady Macduff calls her little son a bird once, and he to himself twice (4.2). This scene also mentions ways to trap a bird, such as with nets, lime, pitfalls, and gin (4.2.34-35). But there is also the indirect reference to the owl as an "obscure bird" and to the martlet, both of which shall be discussed below (2.3.52; 1.6.4). Thus, Shakespeare not only includes birds but also their attributes as illustrations for his characters.

Shakespeare sets up his first avian symbol in the opening act. The battle is winding down, and the success of one great man is being discussed. Macbeth, a general along with Macduff and Banquo, is described by a messenger as being a noble, kingly bird: an eagle (1.2.34-35). The eagle is a large predatory bird, territorial and fierce. Such a description is fitting for Macbeth, a defender of his country and his king. The messenger giving the account mentions that just when the battle was soon to be won, new enemy recruits came against Macbeth, Banquo, and their men. When asked if this "dismay'd" the captains, the messenger replies with a joke saying, "As sparrows eagles, or the hare the lion." (1.2.34-35). Obviously, a lion would not fear a rabbit, and neither would an eagle shy from a tiny sparrow. Macbeth and the other Thanes are symbolized as eagles, showing them to be both noble and fierce. Macdonwald, on the other hand, is described as just the opposite. He is a common sparrow, a tiny bird. He is harmless, more of an irritation than a worrisome creature to a man who has a fighting spirit, like Macbeth. Thus, we get a snapshot into the character of Macbeth, and even his fellow Thanes.

Soon after this initial use, the sparrow is mentioned again and described with a similarly mild nature to depict a scene's atmosphere. King Duncan, who is approaching Macbeth's castle with Banquo, comments on the "pleasant air" surrounding it. So too, Banquo observes the serene land around him and comments on how it is warm and filled with little birds called martlets (1.6.3-8). These little birds are a variety of sparrow; and, as previously mentioned, they are harmless. Banquo remarks that they are "temple-haunting," that is, birds that make their homes among temples—perhaps referencing the Psalmist who spoke of birds making their nests in God's temple—commending the air around the home to be peaceful, for these birds only nest where "the air is delicate" (1.6.3-10).[2] The presence of the peaceful-nesting birds announces at the entrance of Macbeth's castle that this is a place of safety and life. The air, too, that Duncan mentions could also be a reference to the birds that fill it, which he notes "nimbly and sweetly recommends itself" (1.6.2). These birds symbolize the peace and safety found in this dwelling, even life itself, as the bird only makes its "procreant cradle" where the air is safe (1.6.8).

Yet life will not be found here long, and the presence of these martlets may be as deceptive as some characters in the play. In fact, another name for martlet is martin, which during "the sixteenth and seventeenth centuries, a kind of slang term for a 'dupe' was 'martin.'"[3] Thus, Shakespeare likely intended for his audience to see through the bird's innocent nature and foresee the deception coming.[3] Only lines before, a messenger of death came to this place and forecast the deaths of those men who had just been speaking of the seemingly peaceful dwelling. Lady Macbeth, who moments before finished reading the message from her husband, is informed by a servant that King Duncan will soon be at her home to rest. The bird she chooses to name the messenger is a raven (1.5.35-37).

According to Hazlitt, in his book *Faiths and Folklore of the British Iles*, the raven is a messenger of terrible things, a bad omen, and a forewarner of death.[4] He quotes another when he says, "by ravens both publick and private calamities and death have been portended."[4] Again, he states, "Private men have been forewarned of their death by ravens, …a messenger of death," naming Cicero as one such man forewarned.[4] Hazlitt even goes as far as to say that "the croaking of a raven" is to be included among "omens," and that if one "hears a raven croak from the next roof, he at once should make his will."[4] Thus, by croaking his hoarse message to his mistress, this raven brings the dispatch of death for the King. So where it was thought that the very presence of a raven is a warning that some great calamity will happen, we see that only moments after gaining the knowledge of her King's imminent arrival, Lady Macbeth contrives a plan that will bring about his downfall (1.5). Shakespeare displays his knowledge of commonly held superstitions of that time by using such symbols within his writing to foreshadow events for his audience.

Shakespeare also includes a smaller bird of prey: a kite. This bird is a variety of falcon – a small, swift bird. A falcon is mentioned separately in the play, but only to note the tremulous reaction of nature to Macbeth's evil deeds when an evil owl "hawk'd" the bird of prey (2.4.13-14). Macbeth mentions a kite first when talking to the ghost of Banquo when he says, "Our graves must send / Those we bury back, our monuments / Shall be the maws of kites." (3.4.71-73). These lines show the flesh-eating nature of a kite, even going so far as to say that they will eat the flesh of people, their mouths becoming the graves of men. But later in the play, Macduff uses a kite to represent the character of Macbeth. Distraught over the deaths of his family, he calls Macbeth a "hell-kite" (4.3.217). While no such bird truly exists, the use of hell amplifies Macduff's anger toward Macbeth and highlights the destructive nature of Macbeth, who murdered his family "at one fell swoop" (4.3.219). Such wording creates an image of a great bird of prey swooping down to catch some unsuspecting creature to feast upon. Once again, this harkens back to Macbeth's statement, "our monuments / shall be the maws of kites," for the graves and lasting testimony of the Macduff family shall be in the mouth of Macbeth and in the bellies of the birds that consume them (3.4.71-73).

Some birds are mentioned just long enough to provide an insult and perhaps show the lunacy of Macbeth. Towards the end of the play, right when Macbeth is caged in his fortress and nearly all have abandoned him, he insults a servant calling him a "cream-fac'd loon" with a "goose look" (5.3.11-12). In addition to being called a little bird and son of the wren, Macduff's son is called an egg just before he is murdered (4.2.79). While this is somewhat odd or even humorous at first glance, knowing the effort Shakespeare seems to have taken to include avian references, this little insult seems fitting. Moreover, it highlights the cowardice of Macbeth who hunts not only harmless "chickens" but even innocent and defenseless children: a little clutch of eggs in their nest that were dearly loved by their parents. Though here the chicken is referenced for its harmlessness, another one — a rooster — appears earlier. Here, this bird crows to announce the dawn and signal the betrayal of a servant of his master (2.3.20). In folklore, the devil was to fear crowing, an extrapolation from the biblical account.[5] Yet a black cockerel was associated with witchcraft and devilry.[6,7] Similarly, a harpier, or harpy, cries at the start of Act IV when the three witches are making an evil brew before the arrival of Macbeth (4.1.3). In folklore and mythology, harpies were considered to be half woman and half bird, or even a witch turned owl.[8]

Prior to the revelation of the death of his family, Macduff's lady appears on stage while talking to her son, her little bird (4.2). She is currently, and rightly so, feeling abandoned by her Lord, but calls herself a wren who, though tiny, "will fight" (4.2.8-11). The wren, as described in Hazlitt's book, was known as a "little King" or simply "king" by the Greeks and Spaniards, respectively.[9] The Latins, Danish, and Italians referred to the bird as "king," "fowl king," and "little king" as well.[9] Therefore, Macduff must be kingly, or at least noble, in nature to be the mate of a wren. Hazlitt also mentions that the wren "though of such diminutive bulk, harasses the eagle, who holds sway over all other birds."[9] Many other cultures also title this little bird with kingly titles, and even the druids deemed the little wren as "king of all the birds."[9]

Initially, Macbeth was described as a great eagle who was not bothered by little birds, such as sparrows. But here, it is shown that some little birds are an annoyance to what men typically consider the ruler of the birds. The cultural references show the reality of the play's situation. This eagle appears to be more than a little agitated by such a small bird, for he goes to kill them. Furthermore, Macbeth's bird of character changes from an eagle to an owl, the bird that Lady Macduff titles him with (4.2.11). As Macduff later finds out, all of his "pretty chickens and their dam" were killed by Macbeth (4.3.218-219). Apparently, some little birds do get caught in the "net" and "lime" (4.2.34-35). And yet, he and his family are thematically tied to the wren, foreshadowing the final confrontation between Macbeth and Macduff.

Now, some birds appear in *Macbeth* to reveal what people are, not by characterization, but by fulfilling their folklore roles. Such is the case for birds that can speak. After learning of Banquo's death and being visited by the ghost of his murdered friend, Macbeth worries that some natural truth-teller will bear witness to his crimes (3.4.124-127). Besides the possibility of stones, trees, or prophets, he fears that three little birds will open their maws and let his secret

175

deeds of darkness out. These birds are the magpie, the chough, and the rook. All three of these birds are known to be chatterers or to possess the capability of repeating words.

The chough, of the family of crows and rooks, is known by its chatter.[10] In fact, to label someone as a chough would be to call them a chatterer.[10] Evidently, this revealer of tales is not a bird that Macbeth wants near him. In the same way, a magpie by its talk can alert a person that someone is near.[11] Its chattering is also considered an omen but with mixed results; those who have something to hide should avoid these birds.[11] Macbeth in this scene says that all these birds reveal "the secret'st man of blood" (3.4.127). It is here that he realizes that it is not just the spiritual but also the natural world that has the power to speak up about his wrongdoings. He cannot hide.

Yet one bird does hide in the background among the rest, which is fitting for his character. That is the dove, found in Malcolm. His name is derived from Máel Coluim, which meant disciple of St. Columba, whose name means dove.[12] This innocent bird has long been a symbol of peace, which is right for the prince who avoids conflict yet still strives for peace in his homeland. Though the bird never shows up directly by name, it is fitting that the king of the play has a name that originates with a bird.

But out of the many birds included in *Macbeth*, the owl is the most frequent. This is a very particular bird. The fowl takes on a handful of names in the play, but always the same role: that of ill omen. Within Macbeth, the owl is called a "fatal bellman," an "obscure bird"—obscure in that it is hidden in the night but also that it portends evil tidings and is itself a sign of evil—and "night's black agents" (2.2.4-5; 2.3.52; 3.2.53). The owl makes its first entrance with the death of King Duncan (2.2.4). In the scene prior, Macbeth remarks that a bell invites him to kill his King; the following scene contains Lady Macbeth, who calls the owl the "fatal bellman, /

Which gives the sternest good-night" that invites the listener to death (2.2.4-5). In the play, it is also said to kill a falcon when it normally feasts on mice, which would show an upset in nature, and consequently, in Macbeth (2.4.11-14).

The owl has been a decidedly bad omen since the time of the Romans, specifically the "screech-owl at midnight."[13] On the other hand, the Greeks associated the owl with wisdom.[14] Perhaps Macbeth and his lady's fear of the owl's presence is due to the owl's wisdom, for it knows what they have done. Moreover, its presence also meant that some fatal occurrence would happen, which is why many "ancients held owls in the utmost abhorrence."[13] Much like the raven, it brought death. Thus, Lady Macbeth likens the shriek of the owl to that of the bellman's bell. Just as the bells ring in the hour of rest, so too does the "sternest good-night" of the owl call the hour of death's sleep. The owls in *Macbeth* are also called "night's black agents," and Pliny called the owl the "funeral owl and monster of the night" (3.2.53).[13] And as one more fitting inclusion, the witches, just before Macbeth visits them, create some sort of horridness in their cauldron with many baneful ingredients. One such ingredient is the wing of a howlet—a baby owl (4.1.17). It is fitting also that the wing of a baby owl is included in this brew. We can compare how Macbeth is being used in the witches' schemes to that baby owl being used in their wicked brew. He is just a piece of their machinations.

Thus, owls are in every way a symbol of evil in this play and foretellers of destruction. While Lady Macduff is lamenting the loss of her Lord, she calls Macbeth an owl that will come in and attack her "nest" (4.2.10-11). This black agent makes war against the wren and swiftly brings about her death (4.2.11). Indeed, there is such a thing as an eagle owl.[13] Before, Macbeth was called an eagle, then later an owl. And in killing the family of a second friend, he takes on elements of both. He is an ignoble king seeking the deaths of his subjects, his children. His presence is no longer safe, but instead, one of bad omen, bringing destruction wherever he haunts.

But neither the owl nor the ignoble eagle will be permitted to reign. This play seeks resolution, for wrongs to be made right, for evil to be overcome by good; for madness from patricide and for nobility in kingship. And the wren is allowed, though small he be, to overcome the mighty eagle owl. In the final moments of the play, Macduff hunts down Macbeth and makes right known. Macbeth is punished for his sins against Macduff's family, against the people of Scotland, against his King, and against God. And with the wren triumphing, so does right.

For anyone unfamiliar with bird folklore and who is not specifically looking for such creatures, the birds in *Macbeth* can be quickly overlooked in the greater scope of the story, a mix of history and fable. However, their presence brings a greater depth to this story. But imagery, symbolism, and characterization are only appreciated as they are understood. Each bird in *Macbeth* carries with it a symbolic meaning. Without them, the play would carry its story but would not have the same depth of meaning or beauty. Shakespeare's birds are not accidental. Understanding these birds and their meanings symbolically and historically is essential to a reading of *Macbeth*.

References

1. Spurgeon, C. F. (1935). *Shakespeare's Imagery and What it Tells Us.* . Cambridge: Cambridge University Press. 48.
2. Psalm 84:3. *Holy Bible: New International Version.* Grand Rapids: Zondervan, 1984.
3. Spurgeon, 188-9.
4. Hazlitt, W C. *Faiths and Folklore of the British Isles.* Vol. II. New York: Benjamin Bloom, Inc., 1965. 507-8. II vols.
5. Campbell, John Gregorson. Superstitions of the Highlands & Islands of Scotland. United Kingdom, J. MacLehose and sons, 1900. 287, 294.
6. Russell, Jeffrey. *Witchcraft in the Middle Ages.* Cornell University Press. 1972. 216.
7. Encyclopedia of Superstitions, Folklore, and the Occult Sciences of the World: A Comprehensive Library of Human Belief and Practice in the Mysteries of Life .... (1903). United States: J. H. Yewdale & sons Company. 1247.
8. Angell, Tony. *The House of Owls.* New Haven & London: Yale University Press, 2015. 77.
9. Hazlitt, 665-6.
10. "Chough." 1. a.-b. *The Oxford English Dictionary.* 2nd ed. 1933. 385.
11. Hazlitt, 383.
12. Muhr, Kay, and Ó hAisibéil, Liam. The Oxford Dictionary of Family Names of Ireland. United Kingdom, OUP Oxford, 2021.
13. Hazlitt, 468-9.
14. Angell, 72.

Bibliography

Adamnanus; Huyshe, Wentworth. *The Life of Saint Columba (Columb-Kille): A.D. 521-597, Founder of the Monastery of Iona and First Christian Missionary to the Pagan Tribes of North Britain.* Ireland, Routledge, 1922. xiii-lvi, 136-38, 242-44.

The American College Dictionary. 1958.

Angell, Tony. *The House of Owls.* New Haven & London: Yale University Press, 2015. 72, 77.

Barlow, Frank. *Edward the Confessor.* United Kingdom, University of California Press, 1984. xv-xvii, 201-02, 270.

Black, George F. *The Surnames of Scotland: Their Origin, Meaning, and History.* The New York Public Library, 1946.

Campbell, John Gregorson. *Superstitions of the Highlands & Islands of Scotland.* United Kingdom, J. MacLehose and sons, 1900. 287, 294.

"Chough." 1. a.-b. *The Oxford English Dictionary.* 2nd ed. 1933. 385.

"couplet". The Editors of Encyclopaedia Britannica. *Encyclopedia Britannica.* 4 Feb. 2020.

Crawfurd, R. H. P. *The King's Evil.* United Kingdom: Clarendon Press. 1911.

Dyce, Alexander, ed. *A General Glossary to Shakespeare's Works.* Boston: Dana Estes and Company. 1904.

Encyclopedia of Superstitions, Folklore, and the Occult Sciences of the World: A Comprehensive Library of Human Belief and Practice in the Mysteries of Life .... Vol. III. United States: J. H. Yewdale & sons Company. 1903. 1247.

Harper, Douglas, ed. *The Online Etymology Dictionary.*

Hazlitt, W C. *Faiths and Folklore of the British Isles.* Vol. II. New York: Benjamin Bloom, Inc., 1965. 382-83, 468-470,507-8. II vols.

"heroic couplet". The Editors of Encyclopedia Britannica. *Encyclopedia Britannica.* 18 Oct. 2019.

Holinshed, Raphael. Abraham Fleming. *The History of Scotland, An Electronic Edition (English).* Perseus Digital Library.

Holinshed, Raphael. *Holinshed's Chronicles of England, Scotland, and Ireland in Six Volumes.* Vol V. London. 1808.

Holy Bible: New International Version. Grand Rapids: Zondervan, 1984.

Jamieson, John, et al. *Jamieson's Dictionary of the Scottish.* Edinburgh: W.P. Nimmo, 1867.

Lewis, Samuel. *A Topographical Dictionary of Scotland: Comprising the Several Counties, Islands, Cities, Burgh and Market Towns, Parishes, and Principal Villages, with Historical and Statistical Descriptions: Embellished with Engravings of the Seals and Arms of the Different Burghs and Universities.* United Kingdom, S. Lewis and Company, 1851.

Lower, Mark Antony. *Patronymica Britannica: A Dictionary of the Family Names of the United Kingdom.* United Kingdom, J.R. Smith, 1860.

"Macbeth (Folio 1, 1623)." *Internet Shakespeare Editions.* University of Victoria.

"Modern (Modern)." *Internet Shakespeare Editions.* University of Victoria.

Muhr, Kay, and Ó hAisibéil, Liam. *The Oxford Dictionary of Family Names of Ireland*. United Kingdom, OUP Oxford, 2021.

Russell, Jeffrey. *Witchcraft in the Middle Ages*. Cornell University Press. 1972. 216.

Shakespeare, William, and David M. Bevington. "Macbeth." *The Complete Works of Shakespeare*. 5th ed. New York: Pearson Longman, 2004. Print.

Spurgeon, C. F. (1935). *Shakespeare's Imagery and What it Tells Us.* . Cambridge: Cambridge University Press.

Webster's New World College Dictionary. Fourth ed., 1999.

Whyte, Donald. *Scottish Surnames*. Edinburgh: Birlinn. 2000.

Index

Made in the USA
Monee, IL
09 May 2024

8cbcdc02-be2a-4719-8547-f65028fb74b8R01